"Sprung From Hell"

"Sprung From Hell"

Based on the true story of one Biker's journey through hell on earth into the arms of Love

Dorian Hollaway

Xulon Press

Xulon Press
2301 Lucien Way #415
Maitland, FL 32751
407.339.4217
www.xulonpress.com

© 2020 by Dorian Hollaway

All rights reserved solely by the author. The author guarantees all contents are original and do not infringe upon the legal rights of any other person or work. No part of this book may be reproduced in any form without the permission of the author. The views expressed in this book are not necessarily those of the publisher.

Printed in the United States of America.

ISBN-13: 978-1-6322-1758-5

Contents

Preface & Introduction ♦ ix

Bastard Child ♦ 1

Mother Steps Up ♦ 24

School Days ♦ 46

Motorcycles ♦ 59

My Heroes ♦ 72

Last Shred of Innocence Stolen ♦ 78

Rescued ♦ 92

Life Lessons Learned ♦ 07

Biker World ♦ 120

No Longer a Victim ♦ 135

Boys Ranch ♦ 149

"Sprung From Hell"

Runnin' Red Eye ♦ 162

Soldier Boy ♦ 173

Settling Down ♦ 187

Colors and Nam ♦ 202

Pride Before the Fall ♦ 221

Germany and Fatherhood ♦ 241

Hit Rock Bottom ♦ 255

Punching God in the Face ♦ 280

Beauty From Ashes ♦ 300

Birth of a Ministry ♦ 315

Leaving a Legacy ♦ 328

Preface & Introduction

Dear reader,

I'm glad you have chosen to take this journey with Kenner and me. Kenner was raised with lies that robbed him of the truth, expressed in scripture, that he was fearfully and wonderfully made and that the God of the universe knit him together in his mother's womb. His birth was no mistake. Kenner fell prey to the one thing that comes naturally to the enemy. When he lies he speaks from his very nature. Only the truth of God's word can counter the lies of the enemy to set people truly free.

"Sprung From Hell"

There are countless other stories of people in seemingly unbearable situations. Many of these people are children who are at the mercy of the adults around them. This is definite proof that we live in a fallen world. The only thing holding the evil at bay are the believers, filled with the Holy Spirit of God, who reside here. Once God calls us all home, there won't be anything left to stop it.

The fallen state of this world causes misery for everyone. But, this is not a story of despair and disheartenment it is a story of hope and deliverance. No one is beyond God's love. He raised Kenner up and brought him through all the pain and oppression so that his story could reach those who would not be reached by traditional means.

It is my hope and Kenner's that those held in the bondage of the enemy's lies will be led to freedom in Jesus and experience the beauty only He can bring from the ashes.

I'd like to thank the Blood Knights Motorcycle Ministry for teaching me about protocol and for accepting my family and me into their ranks and their hearts.

♦ 1 ♦

Bastard Child

AS A RESULT OF TWO WORLD wars our nation was left in a state of ruin. The great depression had ended, according to Washington, but it still had its claws in the lives of most people. During this time there was a mass influx of migrant farmers and laborers into Oklahoma in search of work in the cotton fields. Many of these workers were war widows with small children.

They settled in large, government subsidized encampments called Shanty

Towns. They were made up of row upon row of shacks built out of scrap lumber and tar paper or anything else they could find. It was frigid and wet in the winter and dry and dusty in the summer. The air was always thick with wood smoke from a hundred cooking fires. Grime and soot covered everything filling every crevice and penetrating every pore. The shacks, the clothes, the people, even the few trees were gray and colorless. Life moved along at a grueling pace marked by desperate striving, abuse and human pain. It was in one of these encampments that my Grandmother and Granddaddy lived.

My father was a young Native American full of pride in his heritage and anger for the way his people had been treated. He was tall and solidly built with hair as black as a crow's wing. He wore his hair long and tied back with a piece of leather. His jaw was strong and square and his complexion dark and smooth. He had eyes so dark they were almost black, smoldering beneath the surface like two burning coals. His family was struggling to survive, like everyone else. He was sent to work in the milk factory to help earn money. My mother, Cara Jean, was one of 19 children born to my grandparents. One of her daily chores was fetching milk from the factory. That is where she met my father. He was 18 and she was 20. Young people, in that day, as now, sought to find some reason beyond the hopelessness of their existence by filling the void with human closeness. My parents' ill-fated romance resulted in an unwed and unwanted pregnancy. This was greatly frowned upon in that day. When significance and human worth are so scarce, any scrap of dignity seems invaluable. It was very important to my Grandmother that her family not be shamed. So, they were forced to marry so that I would have a legitimate name. In spite of this effort to legitimize my birth, I was labeled a bastard from the start.

My father's Native American name, Keñor, which means, "the color of the sky at sunset", was not acceptable in the white community, so my Grandmother gave him an English name; Kenner Doniel Knox Eugene Weaver. Someone in authority said he could only have 3 names, so he chose Doniel Knox and I became Kenner Eugene Weaver born 6/7/42. Kenner was a variation of Keñor, however I did not find out about my Native American heritage until many years later.

My father was a heavy drinker and a violent man. Shortly after my birth my mother became pregnant again. My father flew into a blind rage and beat my mother with an iron skillet till she had a miscarriage and lost my twin baby sisters. Granddad told him if he laid a hand on her again he would be shot. Father knew enough to take him seriously. He left to join the Army. They were divorced and my mother began a life of prostitution in the big city in order to survive. I don't know if she preferred this life or was forced into it because of not being allowed to return home since she had brought shame to the family.

I was taken to live with my grandparents in Shanty Town. They lived in a two room wooden shack with a shed built on to the side. It was actually a fine house by Shanty standards. The main room was about 12' x 16' with a large, rock fireplace dominating one wall. The ancient boards moaned and groaned like a grumpy old man. This is where the cooking was done. Grandmother did most of the cooking. In the winter months we would usually eat together, huddled in the front room against the cold. In the other months meal times depended on work schedules in the fields. The one bedroom was about

"Sprung From Hell"

8' x 8' and had the only closet. The woodshed, which Granddad had added on, was barely wide enough for one bed and twice as long. Grandpa made the shed a room for us boys and the two youngest uncles. The five older boys got the bed and the rest of us got the floor of hard packed dirt. Not the most comfortable of beds but at least it was indoors. At night the shed was filled with the sounds of snoring and wind whistling eerily through the cracks. It smelled of unwashed bodies, old liquor and stale smoke. We crowded together best we could and fought for the few thin blankets we had.

Ours was one of many shanty homes, all standing within just a few yards of each other, next to the cotton fields. Privacy was a luxury we didn't posses. In our little household there were four uncles, two with wives, and six aunts. One of my aunts died when she was twelve. Uncle Ross was the oldest. He became the head of the household when Granddad passed away. He had a boy and three girls. The boy was a mama's boy and kept me in trouble most of the time. One of the girls hung around with us boys and got in as much trouble as we did. Uncle Ray had two boys and a girl. They didn't spend a lot of time with us. Uncle Fred had a boy and a girl. They lived with us. Freddie, my cousin, and I were the black sheep. Aunt Alice said I was the one that ruint her son. Uncle Dave had four boys, two was his and the other two, we're not sure. He also had a girl. He and his wife, along with all the kids lived with us.

Aunt Charlene had three girls. They weren't around much. Aunt Loretta had one girl. She moved to Dallas, because us boys were too naughty for her little daughter. Aunt Mabel was miss talented. She hadn't started having children yet. Then there was Aunt Cheryl, she too was a home child. Aunt Rose had six

"Sprung From Hell"

boys and three girls. Then, a course, there was mother. Most of the girls never went passed 8th grade, and most were married between 6th and 8th grade.

The unmarried ladies got the bedroom, with Grandmother. The married couples slept in the living room. You can see that there was no place for privacy. Most everyone in Shanty Town knew everyone's business. There was a certain understanding, like honor among thieves that nobody interfered with anyone else's family. We all knew what was going on around us and we all knew it wasn't right, but to say anything about anyone else meant they could say something about you too, so nobody said anything. The unspoken vow of silence held us all in a prison of suffering that perpetuated itself from generation to generation.

Grandpa died when I was very young so, I don't remember him. Folks say he was well respected. He was a member of the Volunteer Fire Dept. and a Mason. He was known as a very religious man. After he passed away my uncles took up making "Oklahoma Red Eye". Prohibition had ended in 1933 and the Great Depression was officially over, but the land of the free and home of the brave was still in the midst of a severe recession. Bootleggin was definitely illegal. Oklahoma was a dry state. There were companies that made legal whiskey, but poor folks couldn't afford it. You could buy a bottle of Red Eye for a dollar where as a bottle of legal liquor would cost three and a half dollars. Beer was bootlegged too. A bottle of bootlegged beer was ten cents and from the store you'd pay fifty five cents. That was a lot of money back then.

We kept the still hidden in a near by dried up river bed. The red-eye was made from potato mash. Rotten potatoes were mashed together and left to ferment to create the sour mash. It was then distilled, producing the Red Eye. The mash from the previous batch was mixed with more potatoes and the process continued. Much like the starter used in making sour dough bread.

Although it was illegal, the local authorities would tend to turn a blind eye to our business. Behind the scenes crime syndicates and law makers worked to keep the state dry so that they could maintain their control of the monopoly. Local law enforcement received kickbacks in exchange for protection. Much of the business was conducted within plain sight of the police station. This served to deter any local thieves seeking to rob us of our profits.

A good deal of the business was conducted across state lines as well. This was dangerous because most bootleggers avoided paying protection money to the authorities in the states or counties they traveled through. This would have eaten too much into the profits. Often we paid runners who had nothing to do with the actual bootlegging. It required a relatively new car with a suspension strong enough to carry or pull the heavy load. And any one vehicle could only be used a few times before it would be recognized by the police. It was more cost effective to pay someone a significant enough amount so they were willing to take the chance a few times, and then switch to someone else.

The "family business" was what kept us from starving when the cotton crop failed, for whatever reason. Grandmother did not condone the making of liquor but she allowed it because it brought in money to the family. I can remember pulling a little, red wagon down the street to deliver jars of Red Eye to our friends and neighbors as gifts.

"Sprung From Hell"

At the age of four I started my drinking career. The reason I know this is because I found out when I was older that my uncles used the younger children to test the Red Eye to see if it was fit for sale. Grandmother wouldn't allow those younger than four to be used. If it made us sleepy it was good if it gave us diarrhea then it was not sellable. So, for my fourth birthday my present was a good strong drink. It set fire to my throat and burned all the way to my stomach. I coughed and choked at first, which was apparently hilarious to my uncles. Soon though, I learned to look forward to the warmth in my tummy and the fuzzy feeling in my head. It made me feel like I could take on anything and win or at least I didn't care so much if I lost. From there it was off and running. I knew I was hooked when I was five because I would sneak out at night to drink. All the uncles and aunts, but two, had children around my age, so you can see how the sampling came in. There were plenty of guinea pigs to choose from.

I was a handsome child. I had black hair, like my father, although Grandmother kept it cut short. Unlike my father I have light brown eyes. I was always tall for my age and though I was skinny I was strong, due to lots of hard work. I stayed in trouble most of the time. As a result of my early exposure to the adult world in addition to drinking I also started smoking and cussing. My uncles and older cousins were my examples. The other families in our community were pretty much the same as mine. Children were seen as property and expected to earn their keep. We were to be seen and not heard, to speak only if spoken to, and to obey, without question, anyone older than us. There was no attempt at sheltering us from the harsher aspects of life. As a matter of fact they were forced upon us by those who should have protected us. We had to grow up fast or die trying.

The only room that was not used for sleeping was the cellar unless someone did a no-no. We boys would be sent to the cellar for the smallest of offenses. For serious offenses the girls got a switch, but us boys learned early on what a belt and a razor strap felt like. Each blow could be felt through our clothes, but more often than not we were stripped down to our skivvies so every strap mark stung like fire and left marks that lasted for days. The beating usually went on till blood was drawn. Then we would be sent to the cellar to think about our sins.

The cellar was about 15' from the house and about three-fourths underground. It had a concrete roof with a heavy, wooden door that pulled open. It was always damp and cold no matter what the temperature was outside. There was no light except what came through the cracks in the door. Inside was not very big but to a child, in the dark it seemed there were mysterious depths that could not be seen in the day light. There were wooden shelves where Grandmother stored canned goods and various crates and barrels. Just about anyone older than me could send me to the cellar for any reason. It was usually one of my uncles or older cousins.

I don't remember how old I was the first time I got sent there, I only know it looked to me like a bottomless pit that would be my grave. I felt so tiny and helpless as I was hauled down into the deep, darkness. I tried to pull away, but my uncle's large hand enclosed my thin arm in a viselike grip. My feet only slid out from under me. I cried and begged not to be left there alone. "Please! I promise I'll be good", I screamed as I tried to climb the steps up only to be shoved back down. The door slammed engulfing me in darkness and terror. I climbed the steps and pounded on the rough wood till my knuckles were raw. "Please, don't leave me here".

I knew there were bugs and rats hiding in the darkness. I could imagine their glowing eyes and sharp teeth. The dampness seeped into my clothes and I shivered violently, both from fear and cold. Tears flowed down my cheeks. Every sound was magnified by the horror that gripped my young imagination. I eventually fell asleep curled into a tiny ball on the top step with whimpering gasps shaking my small frame. I was left there all night. When the pale light of dawn shown around the crack in the door I awoke with my muscles stiff and my heart rejoicing that I had made it through the night. As time passed it seemed to me that I got sent there more often than anybody else no matter how I begged and pleaded.

Bastard Child

I learned early on that my identity was dictated by the fact that I was a bastard child. It was made clear to me that I was damaged goods. I was not loved or even wanted. I was a burden that no one cared to bear, but they didn't know how to be rid of me. Because I was left handed I was also considered a hellion or child of the devil. My self worth was trampled to nothing. I was worthless, a half-wit child incapable of learning or doing anything good. I grew each day not knowing what it felt like to be cared for.

Because I believed that my family's opinion of me must be right I got into a lot of fights. Although I was small I carried a load of hurt and anger that would have crippled a grown man. This only served to reinforce the belief that I was no good. One time, I remember, I broke Frankie's front teeth. Thank God they were his baby teeth. As each stroke of the belt fell I was told, "You are a

"Sprung From Hell"

no-good-for-nuthin, half-wit, bastard. You're not worth the trouble. We'd all be better off without you." I cried myself to sleep in the cellar once more with throbbing pain from the lashes and the words. Sometimes Aunt Cheryl would be sent to read to me from the Bible about how I was evil. She hated it and me because she felt I was causing her to be punished. She hates me to this day because of that.

Grandmother was very much a hard shell Baptist though I never knew her to set foot inside a church, but then, my first years I thought our house was a church. She would read the Bible all the time, mostly the Old Testament. Her voice would resound with reverent authority and cast fear into our young hearts as she proclaimed the righteous judgment of God on sinners. To me the Bible was a scary book, all about punishment. God was unloving and unforgiving and if He did exist I was sure He didn't like me.

I never heard of Jesus until years later when I joined the military.

The person I looked up to the most was my uncle Dave. He was only about Six or seven years older than me and he liked the same things I did; cars and building things. He was so cool. Everyone liked him because he was good looking and could be charming when he wanted to. If I could be like him maybe people would like me too. He let me hang around as long as I was useful. I was his gofer. This is how I learned about motors. Bikes weren't a well known thing then, but if they had been around, Dave would have been hard-core. Till James Dean came into my life, I lived to be just like my uncle Dave.

When I was four I started working in the cotton fields too. One reason they put us kids to work was, so they could keep an eye on us and we earned the family a little extra money. We started work at

5:00 AM and worked till sundown, about 8:00 PM. We got paid by how much our bags of cotton boils weighed. It was easier to pick the boils than the cotton itself. We just broke off the whole bulb. It was still hard work though. The sun tormented us with its intensity. The hard ground soaked up the heat and then radiated it back on us. The glare reflected off the white of the cotton and stung my eyes. Rubbing them didn't help because the grit from my hands would just transfer to my eyes. It felt like ground up glass scraping the inside of my lids. Sweat poured down my face and ribs soaking my clothes and making them stick to me. That at least provided some fleeting relief when a rare breeze would blow across the fields. At first my hands were rubbed raw. They would crack and bleed and smart something fierce from the sweat and dirt. One time I cried to my grandmother because they stung so bad. She picked up a handful of dirt and started rubbing it into my palms. I cried harder and then she slapped me hard across the face and said, "Stop your whining and get back to work." Eventually they became rough and calloused so they didn't hurt so much.

I thought I found a short-cut once. I put rocks in my bag. When I took it to be weighed it was 60lbs. The man didn't fall for it. He dumped my sack and threw it at me. "I don't have time for pranks", he hollered. He called one of my aunts who was working nearby and sent me back into the field. Only now I had to work along-side her so she could watch me. "Can you do anything right?" she asked. The half-wit was a burden with ever increasing weight. As punishment, I didn't get paid anything for that whole day of work. That got me another whippin and more time in the cellar.

On top of working in the fields I also had the chores of making sure the firebox was filled and the beds were made and picked up from the floor of the shed. There wasn't much time for playing but we took advantage of what time we did have. My best friends were Billy and Bubba. Billy was a bit older than us, so he got interested in girls pretty soon and didn't hang with us much anymore. Bubba was closer to me than any of my family. One of our favorite things to do was make kites out of old newspaper. We would collect pieces of string and tie them together to make our kite go as high as we could. I would imagine what it would be like if I could fly far away from Shanty Town. I wondered if the entire world was the same or if there were places where I wouldn't be a half-wit bastard.

We never got new toys not even at Christmas. The only way I ever knew it was Christmas was that Grandmother would kill a chicken and we would get hand-me-down clothes from the neighbor. I found out they were hand-me-downs when the neighbor boy made fun of me because I was wearing his old clothes. Bubba beat him up for that.

Some of the adults would get presents. Uncle Dave got a belt once with a shiny silver buckle. It was the finest belt I had ever seen. I wished I could have it. When it was used to give Dave a beating with, he cut it up. If there were ever presents of any kind the older kids got them. It was survival of the fittest and the little ones always got left out.

I would make my own toys out of old, broken ones I would find. I made a skateboard once out of a pair of broken roller skates and a piece of board. Bubba and I almost felt like we were flying when we rode it. I found a small hunting knife in a field once. I kept that one to myself. It was my favorite toy for a long time. I whittled and practiced throwing it all the time. I got really good at hitting my mark.

"Sprung From Hell"

One thing we did each get was a pair of brogans. They were shoes made of rough leather on the top and the soles were made of old tires. They had to last us all year but then they were impossible to wear out. You just hoped you didn't grow much because there is nothing more painful than stiff shoes that don't fit. I did get a new pair of cover-alls once, right before first grade. I was so proud because they weren't hand-me-downs. Then I found out that cover-alls were only for poor folks and I got made fun of again.

◆ 2 ◆

Mother Steps Up

IN MY VERY EARLIEST YEARS MY mother never spent much time with me. The fact is I thought she was one of my aunts for years. She would come and go and say she loved me but, that didn't mean much. My mother was a beautiful woman. She was around 5' 7" and had a voluptuous figure that caught the eye of many a man. She had fiery red hair and large sparkling green eyes. She wore bright red lipstick that accentuated the sensuous curve of her lips. She never spoke of my father.

"Sprung From Hell"

Somewhere around the end of my fourth year I was playing out in back of the house when my uncle Ross grabbed me and shoved me in the closet. "You stay in there", he growled at me. I wondered what I had done this time. Then I heard a man shouting my name. I didn't recognize the voice. He was screaming that he had come to get me. I did recognize the way he slurred his words and I knew he was drunk. I couldn't imagine what I had done to make this stranger so angry. I hoped with all my heart that my uncle wouldn't give me to him. I tried to shrink back in the closet as far as I could so if he came to get me out maybe he wouldn't see me. My uncles were yelling at him to get out of their house and don't ever show his sorry face around there again. I heard some scuffling and a crash and then the door slamming. All was quiet for a few minutes then the closet door flew open. I scrunched back in the corner trying to be invisible. I just knew they had finally found a way to be rid of me. Uncle Ross just said, "You can come out now", and walked away. I peeked out around the corner but the stranger was nowhere to be seen. I crept out slowly, ready to run at the first sign of trouble. Everyone seemed to have forgotten that anything out of the ordinary had just happened. Nobody bothered to explain anything to me. Later I heard my aunt Cheryl talking to Aunt Mabel about how the angry stranger had been my father. He had come to take me with him but, they wouldn't allow it because he was a drunk. At that moment I started wondering if I might have wanted to go live with him. Maybe he really wanted me. He was awful scary though. I decided I was better off staying where I was.

Sometimes I dreamed of having a father, although I never knew one that I thought was good. None of my uncles ever showed any real care for their own kids and they certainly had no use for me. I figured all men were mean, angry and selfish. I finally saw what a good father was like when I saw "Leave It to Beaver" on T.V. in 1956. I loved that show and dreamed of having a family like Beaver. All the men I had any encounter with were certainly not anything like Mr. Cleaver.

Even strangers, who walked onto the stage of my life for only a brief moment, played a part in shaping my character. When I was nine or ten, one of the times I lived with my mother, a salesman came to our door selling something. I was playing Tarzan and I had an old towel around my waist. The salesman said,"that boy's too old to be playing in a diaper". My mother replied, "It's not a diaper, he's playing Tarzan". "Well, he looks like he's wearing a diaper". He looked at me as if I were a freak in a side-show. I felt like one

Mother Steps Up

too. Suddenly I was on display, exposed to the cruel opinion of onlookers. My face burned with shame. I never played Tarzan again.

Back to being five, I am now really enjoying the "sample time". It occurred to my mother that it was time for her to begin parenting me. She came and took me to Tulsa, Ok. I don't know if the surprise visit from my father had anything to do with her sudden desire to be a mom. This was actually when I realized that she was my mama. In my heart I dared to hope that life was taking a turn for the better.

I had never seen a motel before but, now I was living in one. Each cottage, as they were called, was two stories tall and had six or eight doors on its front. Rusty stairs with peeling paint were perched precariously on each end. The doors each had a big, red number painted on them. Inside there was one bed with a side table holding a lamp with a torn yellow shade and a small dresser. It smelled kind of like soured milk and cigarette smoke mixed together. The bathroom was indoors, that was different. The floor was smooth and hard. I couldn't say what color it was because it was so stained that the color changed depending on where you looked. The air inside the room was thick and humid. It made everything feel sticky, especially the sheets on the bed.

At night there were red lights casting an unearthly glow on the cracked concrete sidewalks. It was never quiet at night. The place seemed to come to life after dark but, it was sort-of a false life, maybe it couldn't exist in the light. Our room was small but with only two people in it I thought it felt huge. Well, there were only us two except for all the new "uncles" who would come to stay the night. I knew something was off kilter but, I couldn't quite put my finger on it.

Mother Steps Up

Most of the other rooms were being rented by other "business women", like my mama. For the most part, they were nice ladies. Behind their painted eyes and red lips there seemed to be a veil of sadness shrouding their souls. Even their laughter didn't sound right. It was like tears were always on the verge of seeping through. Some of the rooms were vacant so they could be rented out by the hour. The man who owned the establishment stayed mostly out of sight. He just came around in his baggy, tan trousers and stained, sleeveless shirt to collect the rent. His eyes always looked like they hurt and his stomach always spilled out from the top of his trousers like it was trying to escape. He looked greasy all the time and smelled like spoiled bacon but, he never bothered me. If the ladies couldn't pay in cash He'd accept other forms of payment and disappear back into his hole until next rent day.

I met more "uncles" than I thought anyone could have. Mother would make a pallet on the floor, next to the bed, for me while she conducted business. I didn't really understand what was going on but I knew my mama was what they called a prostitute.

D.W. was a regular customer. He was a little older than my mama and not what I would call handsome. He always looked like he'd just woken up in a ditch somewhere and smelled like it too. I didn't like him right from the start. He was real jealous and he beat my mama just about every night. It wasn't that he cared for her and wanted to marry her or anything like that. He was just selfish and wanted her all to himself. I tried to intervene a few times. I didn't want him hurting my mother. But, a five year old's fists don't inflict much damage against a full grown man. Even with all the rage I had built up inside me I was no match for him. I sure tried though. He just shoved me or slugged me or literally threw me out of his way. One of those times I ended up with a big gash in my head. Mother tried to keep me out of it. "This is grown-up stuff and you just don't understand", she would explain. Well, she was right, I didn't understand. I knew she was trying to protect me. It felt good to have someone at least care that I not get hurt. Still it hurt me in a different way. A new pain, that hurt somewhere deep inside me, somewhere you couldn't see it or touch it. The agony was so great sometimes I felt it would crush me. I could feel the bricks of frustration and bitterness being stacked up in my soul. A wall was forming that gathered all my anger into a simmering pool of hatred and at the same time kept other feelings and people out. Letting myself care only made me vulnerable to being hurt again. I had to separate myself from those feelings. I don't believe this was a conscious decision, I think it just happened. A child views life through the lens of feelings and it is rarely a clear picture. I was only five and my immature reasoning only perpetuated the lies I believed about myself and my life. Most nights I just laid on the floor, beside the bed, crying.

There isn't much to do in a motel but, I found things to occupy me. I learned a lot looking into the other windows. Meantime D.W. was getting more angry and aggressive as the days went by. He was jealous of Mama having other customers. He figured out it got to her more if he took out his anger on me. Mother would try to stop him. She put herself between me and him and took the brunt of his beatings for me. They would always end up in the bed. Sex made everything okay; at least that's what I thought for years.

Mother Steps Up

One day the fight was worse than ever. D.W. showed up and he was real drunk. He had a bottle of bleach. He spat out the words, "You love your son more than me". He started coming at me. The hatred I saw in his eyes scared me more than anything I had ever seen before. I could sense that Mother was genuinely afraid too. She snatched me up and ran to Dottie's room. Dottie answered the panicked pounding on her door and knew immediately something was terribly wrong. Mama shoved me inside and spilled the story to her between frantic gasps. "Call the cops", Mama yelled over her shoulder as she ran back to her room. I didn't want her to go back there. I tried to run after her but Dottie grabbed me by the shirt and pulled me back into the room. "Just sit tight while I call the cops", she instructed with a warning finger in my face. I found out later that when Mama returned to our room she found

"Sprung From Hell"

D.W. dead on the floor. He had drunk the bleach. Maybe that's what he planned to do all along, but I couldn't help wondering if it had been intended for me. Oh well, at least he wouldn't be bothering me and mama any more.

I started school in Tulsa. The school there was bigger than the one in Shanty Town. Each grade had a separate class. The six of us kids that lived at the motel didn't attend school very regularly. Our mothers mostly slept during the day. So, left to our own choosing, we stayed home to play. There was one girl, about my age, who I spent most days with. I don't remember her name but, I remember she was pretty and blonde. She always wore two bows in her hair, one on each side of her head. They were different colors to match her dresses. Some days we would play with her dolls. I didn't know how a daddy was supposed to act so; I just pretended we had a family like I wished I had. Other days we would play in the dirt with my cars. She was pretty cool, for a girl. My cars were old matchbox cars I had found. They didn't have any wheels and most of the color had rubbed off but, that didn't matter to us. We had the run of the parking lot. It was our asphalt playground. We didn't mind that it was rough and hot and unforgiving if you fell down on it. In our young minds it was a wonderland of possibilities.

We didn't have much modern stuff so; an ice man would come and bring us ice. It was the Blue Star ice co. The motel was in a horse shoe shape. The ice man would come in at the north end and circle around to the south end before getting up on the highway again. I would hide at the first cottage and meet him at his first stop. At just the right time I would jump on the back and hold on tight. I'd ride around to his last stop and hop off just before he left. I stayed crouched down on the right side so, he couldn't see me. My friend with the blonde hair would join me on my ride sometimes.

On one fateful day we boarded our magic coach ready for an exciting ride. We had no idea what awaited us. As we neared the jump off point we poised on the back ready to leap to safety. As the appointed sight approached the terrifying realization hit, he was not slowing down. I looked frantically for an opportunity to jump but, he continued to gain speed. If we didn't find a way to get off we would soon be on the highway. I looked at my friend and saw the panic in her eyes. She silently begged me to do something. I reacted out of sheer desperation and half shoved, half threw her as far as I could, trying to propel her to safety. Then I jumped with all my might. I knew, as I left the bumper, that I was not going to make it. I saw my friend sprawled on the asphalt as one of the wheels of the truck hit her ankle. I felt the shock of my body slamming into the pavement and heard the sickening sound of bones crunching as the truck ran over both my legs. The red, hot pain seared through every fiber of my being. Then everything went black.

At some point I must have regained consciousness momentarily. I saw Dottie carrying my friend away. There were flashing red and blue lights. Voices all around, I could hear my mama crying. People were everywhere. My brain began to blur from the pain and I passed out again. When I woke up I was in the hospital with braces on both my legs. By the time we returned to the motel my friend had moved away. I don't know how severely she was injured or what ever became of her. I hope and pray, to this day, that she was okay.

I was sent to school with those contraptions on my legs. Children can be so cruel. Perhaps it's because they're too young to have developed the ability to empathize with another person's pain. Perhaps they are only imitating what they have experienced from the adults in their own lives. Whatever the reason, it hurts. The kids made horrible jokes at my expense. They called me embarrassing names and would stand around me laughing at my agony. I wished I could just melt into the ground to escape their brutality. More bricks were added to my inner wall. I refused to go back to school after that. I had proven to be a burden too heavy for Mama to bear. She sent me back to Grandmother.

Now my cousins and old friends didn't want anything to do with me. Even Bubba shunned me. He looked kinda sad about it but, joined right in with the makin' fun. I couldn't understand exactly why. I wondered if he was mad at me for leaving, like I had abandoned him. But, most likely it was because of my braces. I had become an object of shame and for him to associate with me; he would have had to share in my disgrace.

The school in Shanty Town was much smaller than the one in Tulsa. The first through the fourth grade shared one classroom. The smaller kids got picked on anyway just because they were easy targets. I became the whipping boy for them all. Their favorite name for me was "stilt legs".

Teachers were never any help for me. My first grade teacher was Mrs. Dawson. I bet there is a school somewhere that teaches teachers how to look like they just sucked on a sour grape and sound like nails on a chalkboard and to be meaner than a starved dog. They also taught them that a left handed child was a hellion. The offspring of the devil deserves whatever bad treatment comes their way. School was torture.

"Sprung From Hell"

Grandmother pulled me out of school and kept me home. Now, this was not to protect me. She said I was an embarrassment to the family. She tried to home-school me, probably because she felt it was her obligation. I don't know if she ever went to school but, she knew some math and how to read the Bible so, that is what she showed me.

I had those braces on for a total of nine months. They were the loneliest months of my life. I learned that if I was gonna make it I would have to make it alone.

Soon after the braces finally came off we were to have a large family reunion. There would be uncles and aunts and cousins everywhere. There would be bar-b-q and lots of other treats that we rarely enjoyed. Now that I wasn't "stilt legs" anymore maybe they would play with me; my anticipation soared. It would surely be a grand day. Even as my hopes grew my doubts and fears added more bricks to the

Mother Steps Up

wall. My defenses were firmly in place. When one of Aunt Cheryl's kids, named Kelly, thought he had the right to take a toy from me since, I was the half-wit anyway, so I pulled my knife on him. Boy! was he scared. I felt powerful for a fleeting moment. I had found a line of defense against mistreatment. Of course, he went crying to his mama and I got my prize knife taken away.

Aunt Cheryl was livid. She screamed all red in the face and puffing like a steam engine that she had known all along that I was wicked. She would not stand for me being a part of the reunion. Everyone seemed to agree that I would only ruin the day because of my hell bent ways. So, I was locked in the cellar.

This time it was day light at least. The temperature was cool but it was sticky and muggy. Flies were buzzing around my head and ears constantly. I could hear the adults talking and laughing. I could hear the other kids playing and running around. I could smell the savory scent of meat cooking over the fire. My mouth watered and my stomach grumbled. Everyone seemed to have forgotten about me. They were enjoying the day more without me around to cause trouble and embarrassment anyway. I never got anything to eat. I slumped down in the dirt feeling the burden of my own worthlessness pushing me down. Why wasn't I good enough for anyone to love me? Why did I have to be the one born a left-handed bastard? I was only five but someday I would be bigger and then, nobody would ever lock me in the cellar again. Years later I would make good on that promise.

Well, it took some time but, eventually I made friends with Bubba again. He was getting beat on by another neighbor boy. I didn't know what the fight was about but that didn't matter anyway. I jumped in the middle of it and gave that

Mother Steps Up

boy a whipping. Bubba and I were fast friends again.

Now, I don't want you to think I was the only one who ever did anything bad. The other boys got in their share of trouble too. Kelly set fire to the barn and Darren blew up the still once. Mischief was just a part of who we were. When punishment was dished out it was swift and severe. Uncle Ray used a belt but, Uncle Ross preferred a razor strap. They would both draw blood it just took fewer lashes with the razor strap than with the belt.

About this time Mother met R.B. in a bar. Her favorite drink was Falstaff beer and he bought her more than a few. He was a lot calmer sort than D.W. had been. He was surely better groomed and smelled better. They got married and mother came to take me "home". We moved this time to Oklahoma City. We didn't live in a motel this time. R.B. must have had a decent job because we lived in a small house. I actually had my own room.

Mother seemed pleased with herself, like she had achieved some new level of class now that she was a wife. At least R.B. didn't hit her. I almost allowed myself to think things might turn out okay. But, alcohol was still a prevalent part of life. I soon found out that when R.B. was drunk he was more interested in me than in Mother. He came in my room one night. He had a look in his eyes that sent a shiver of fear down my spine. He spoke softly to me about how I was such a handsome young man. His voice reminded me of the hiss of a snake. He lifted the covers off me and started pulling at my clothes. I froze in confusion and horror. Just then Mama walked in. I was suddenly afraid she would be angry with me. The familiar feeling of shame draped over me. But, she wasn't angry with me she was angry with him. She screamed and cussed at him. She said he was "gay". I didn't care if he was happy or not. I just didn't want him touching me.

She took me back to Grandmother. Poor Mama, I think she really tried. She just wasn't any better at being a mom than she was at picking guys. So, back in Shanty Town, a boy of six with more street smarts than a lot of grown men. I should not have known all the things I knew. My childhood was shattered before I'd even lost my baby teeth.

♦ 3 ♦

School Days

MY SIXTH YEAR WAS THE START of another new adventure. Being drunk, having fun, getting into trouble and racing through life. I lived up to my reputation. If you hear something often enough you begin to believe it and you become what you believe. I was a hellion and I acted like it.

Our school was a two story, rectangular, building on a huge patch of dirt set off from the other buildings in town. It rose from the ground, looming like a menacing monster, towering over the

School Days

heads of unsuspecting victims. Once you entered you were at the mercy of the wardens who ran their prison with iron fists. Mrs. Brown was my second grade warden. She was tall, for a woman, and built like a football player. She always wore stiff, dark suits buttoned up to her chin. I don't think she had a neck. The buttons stretched taut over her ample figure. A gray bun perched on top of her head pulled up so tight it stretched the skin on her face. It must have been painful. Maybe that's one reason she was so crabby all the time. She called me New-Gene to make fun of my name. I hated it.

Billy Baird came up with a plan to get her. He brought a package of tacks to school and said we should put them on her chair. He was too chicken to actually go through with it so, I did it. We sat quietly as she entered the classroom. She eyed us with suspicion as she approached her desk. We were trying so hard to suppress our anticipation. Billy almost blew it but I gave him a look that shut him up quick. He clamped his hand over his mouth so hard his knuckles turned white.

She lowered herself cautiously into her chair still looking suspiciously at us and not noticing the tacks. Every muscle in my body tightened waiting for her to bolt up out of her seat. She settled in the chair and then turned her attention to the papers on her desk. We all looked at each other in amazement. Billy's mouth hung open wide enough for a crow to fly in. I shrugged my shoulders in complete confusion. I knew I put them on there and I even double checked to make sure they were all poking up right.

After shuffling through her papers for a few seconds she looked up and announced the lesson number for the day. I looked at Billy and the other guys with a bewildered expression as I slowly opened my book.

What we didn't know was that she was wearing a corset type girdle that extended from her chest halfway down her legs. It was so thick that she never felt the tacks but they stuck tight in the stiff elastic. When she stood to write on the chalk board the dark blue fabric on her back side looked like the night sky dotted with white stars. We could not contain ourselves any longer. Laughter erupted from the whole class like a sudden cloud burst. Her hand flew behind her as if she instinctively knew there was something amiss with her skirt. She turned to the class with fire blazing in her eyes. I had a laugh at that time in my life that resembled machine gun fire. I was completely overcome with the hilarity of the situation and my machine gun was stuck on automatic discharge. I could not have stopped laughing no matter how hard I

"Sprung From Hell"

tried. She spit out my name with venom as she called me to the front of the class. I don't think it would have mattered if I hadn't been the one responsible she would have taken out her rage on me anyway just because she enjoyed making a spectacle of me.

She grabbed my hand and began striking my knuckles with a wooden ruler. She struck with such enthusiasm that the ruler broke after 5 blows. This only served to fuel the fire of my laughter. She looked as if she might explode as she ordered the class to exit the room. I was dragged by one arm into the nearby coat closet. There was a yard stick leaning against the wall. She administered blow after blow to my back and legs. The thin wood started to crack. It broke more with each strike till it splintered into several pieces. At this point I am still laughing. She reached for whatever she could grab and landed on a metal coat hanger. She

School Days

unleashed all her fury on me and continued beating me until I cried out in pain pleading with her to stop. Finally she released her grip and shoved me to the ground. Her chest was heaving from the exertion and she hissed through her teeth for me to go home.

When I arrived home and was asked why I was early I got another beating, this time from Uncle Ray. At least he used a belt rather than the razor strap. The belt didn't sting as much with each lash but I usually got more licks with the belt because it took longer to draw blood. Either way I was sore for about a week after. I never returned to school that year. I had embarrassed the family again.

I was sent to work on the milk farm for the rest of the school term. I worked from sun-up to sun-down feeding the cows and cleaning up after them. It was hard, stinky work. My hands blistered and bled. My muscles all cramped

"Sprung From Hell"

and ached. But, I liked the cows. They were quiet and gentle. I kinda felt safe around them. They didn't care that I was a half-wit, bastard, hellion and I didn't embarrass them. They actually became my friends. I could tell them all my thoughts and feelings. They just listened except for an occasional moo. That wasn't such a bad time.

Before long it was summer time. One day we were playing hide & seek. I thought I found the perfect hiding place. There was an old cedar casket lying on the ground behind the house. Grandmother had bought it to bury Grandpa but then someone gave her a metal one that was much nicer. So, the old cedar one was just sitting there. I crept to the back being careful so no one would see where I went and guess my plan. I crawled inside and closed the door slowly so it wouldn't creak. I felt a chill as soon as the lid shut and I was enclosed in darkness. I squeezed my eyes shut willing my heart to stop thumping. I just knew they could hear it the way it was pounding so loud in my ears. A creepy, panic started to swell in my chest. The realization that I was in a coffin dawned on me. I was just about to abandon my secret hiding place when I heard someone outside. A renewed excitement about winning the game took over with the assurance of getting out of the box soon. But, release was not to come. Freddie locked me in and ran off. Suddenly I was gripped with fear. The walls of the casket started to close in. My throat ached and my chest felt as if a crushing weight was compressing it. I began to scream and thrash around pounding me feet and hands against the wood. I thought I could feel the hot breath of the devil on my neck. The frightening realization came to my mind, "I'm going to hell like Grandmother said would happen". I could hear evil laughter as I pictured the perverse satisfaction on the demons faces as they watched my torment. I don't know how long I was actually in there but I had passed out from exhaustion and the suffocating heat before someone came to let me out. It was supper time and I had been missed at the table. I do recall Freddie getting in trouble for locking me in. He spent some time in the cellar. I got sent to bed with no supper. I didn't much care though. I was too exhausted and nauseated to eat anyway. I felt and probably looked like a drowned rat. I sobbed quietly till I fell asleep. I still fear closed in places to this day.

My uncle Ross took me in that same summer. I'm not certain of the reason. Maybe Grandmother felt he could knock some sense into me, or maybe she was just tired of dealing with me. At any rate, he lived in a one room house with my aunt and cousins. We all slept in the same room. When they had "relations" we

School Days

all heard it. From my days at the motel with Mother I had learned how and what to look at on a woman. I looked at my aunt. That got me in trouble a lot and my cousins too. That summer left scars on my body and my heart.

The summer ended and it was time for school again. There was one teacher I remember who was young and pretty. She was like a flower among a bunch of old thorny branches. She even smelled pretty. Well, due to the fact that I had been exposed to things that awakened certain sensations in my body and mind that I was not mentally or emotionally equipped to deal with wisely I engaged in masturbation at school. One of the mean, ugly teachers caught me. She dragged me unceremoniously through the hall to the office where they called my uncle. When he arrived with my aunt in tow I knew I was in for it. I had really shamed the family this time. He told me to go get the bristle brush from the bathroom. I thought I was going to get a whipping with it. I wish that had been the case. He made me use it on my privates while he and my aunt and the teacher watched. I was so embarrassed. Shame settled over me like a heavy wet blanket. I wished with all my heart he would stop looking at me. "Harder", he demanded, till it burned like fire and I broke down and cried. My mind spun around in a dizzying dance of confusion. Why was sex okay for grownups but so evil for kids? Why did it feel good but warrant such severe punishment? Why was the draw so strong if it brought such shame? I concluded that I was just dirty and messed up.

Well, I was sent back to school for the third grade. Mrs. Travis was the third grade teacher. She was tall but a lot thinner than Mrs. Brown. She always wore a skirt that reached to her ankles

School Days

and a button up blouse starched so stiff it seemed it might break if she made any sudden movements. Her face was long and thin, as were her lips, and dominated by her large nose. Horn rimmed spectacles perched on the tip of it. Somehow her hair was swept up on both sides and formed a stiff, sharp wave at the top of her forehead. She hated me more than Mrs. Brown had. She called me the child of the devil.

It was her mission that year to drive the evil from me that caused me to write with my left hand. I got so many licks on my knuckles that they just stayed swollen and red all the time. I tried to write with my right hand but I just couldn't seem to control the shape of the letters. One afternoon, while the other kids were having recess outside, she decided that would be the day I would be "delivered". For half an hour she stood over me screaming at me and repeatedly striking my hand with her ruler. I was frustrated beyond control. My hand was almost too swollen to even hold onto my pencil and it stung and throbbed like a thousand sharp pins were continually stabbing it.

Finally, in exasperation, she grabbed my left arm and delivered a sharp blow with the edge of the ruler on the side of my arm, consequently breaking both small bones in my forearm. I heard as much as felt the crack. The pain took a couple of seconds to register because I was in shock. When it came it was excruciating. I tried desperately to pull away as I realized she was going to do it again on the other side but that only sent the searing pain shooting up and down my arm. After the second blow she released her grip on me and I sank pitifully into my chair cradling my arm protectively. She stuck her beak of a nose directly into my face and said, "We will see if you can do the devil's work with a broken arm".

School Days

She instructed me to tell my family that I had fallen down on the play ground or she would make my life miserable for the rest of the school year. I believed her so, I did just that and no questions were asked.

Four years later, when my cousin Darren was in her class, she threatened him by saying she had broken my arm and she would do the same to him. He came home and told my uncles. They were mad but didn't ever do anything. It just proved to me once more that I would have to take care of myself because no one else would. Shortly after that I refused to return to school. My education took a turn at that point.

♦ 4 ♦

Motorcycles

I SPENT A LOT OF TIME AT THE still. My uncles were happy to have me around as long as they had work for me to do. Eventually they would get drunk and want to engage in other "activities". There were always girls around who were more than willing to accommodate them. They would send me back to the house. Grandmother would be angry most of the time that I had been down at the still instead of helping her. I usually got sent to the cellar.

Motorcycles

Mother would call every week or so to check on me. She sincerely wanted to be a good mom, I think, but it just wasn't in her. Grandmother would say, "Your mother called today asking about you". I was glad she had called but I didn't feel motherly sentiments for her. She was more like a friend that lived far away.

Well, about this time Uncle Dave found an old Indian Scout. They were bikes that were made before Harleys came on the scene. He told me if I could make it run it was mine. This was the beginning of a whole new passion in my life. I knew he never expected that I would actually get it to run. I saw this as my opportunity to prove that the half-wit could do something worthwhile. I focused all my youthful energies and hopes on that bike.

Now, I didn't have a clue what to do. There was an old black man named Ferd who lived on the other side of the run-off creek. He was a customer of my uncle's. Now, white folks were not supposed to associate with the blacks but I knew he had a son who rode a bike. It was a Harley 175. He seemed my best bet for finding out what I needed to do. Bubba wanted to help too so, we waited till we saw Ferd and Chuck, another oldtimer, sitting on Ferd's porch playing checkers. We snuck up and ducked behind a scraggly bush not quite sure what kind of reception we would get. Ferd knew we were there. He never looked up from the checker board. He just said,"What'er you boys up to? You gonna get a whippin fo sho". I jumped up and said, "What are we gonna get a whippin for?" "Fo comin acrost the crick", he drawled as he jumped two of Chuck's checkers. Chuck banged his fist on the table and declared that Ferd was a cheater. "I aint' neither, you ol' coot", Ferd retorted. Bubba and I took this opportunity to creep up closer while they were distracted. "Yo jus' a so' loser, thas all", Ferd was saying. Chuck just grunted. As we reached the broken down steps they both turned and looked at us. I was amazed that I did not see any anger or hatred in their eyes, only simple questioning. "I got a motorcycle that won't run and I figured you might know what to do", I blurted out. Their eyes lit up as they turned to each other with obvious excitement. But then a look of unrest replaced it. "Wher'd you boys git a bike? Chuck asked suspiciously squinting his eyes at us. "My uncle found it and he gave it to me, but it don't run", I explained. "You wanna help us or not?" I challenged with my fists balled up on my hips. I must have appeared comical because they both started hootin' and slapping their thighs. When they regained control of themselves, they promised to do what they could.

Ferd asked if I had checked the plugs. "What are plugs", I asked. He took his time explaining what they looked like and where to locate them. He told me how to tell if they were good or not. So, trekking back and forth over the creek became a daily practice. The plugs were okay. Next I checked the wires, the fuel line, the carburetor and the head. Every step of the way Ferd and Chuck would patiently explain the purpose for each part and how they worked together to make an engine run. Finally, after exhausting all other possibilities, Ferd decided it must be the O ring. He told me how to remove the bolts that held the jug in place. Then, I had to locate the clamp at the bottom and lift the jug off the engine. When I did it about twenty pieces of something fell out. My heart dropped down into my shoes. I thought I had destroyed it for sure. I ran to Ferd's place. The words tumbling out of my mouth so fast he had to shush me several times before I ended my sad tale with a deep sigh. He giggled at my despair, then explained, "Thas' the O ring, jus like I tol' ya, boy". I asked him where we could get a new one. He said we would make one. "Hog hide's the bes' thing", he said. I knew exactly where to go. There was a slaughter house in town that slaughtered hogs every day. Brad, who I knew from him buying from my uncles too, worked there. I explained to him what I was trying to do. He knew just what I needed. He cut me a 16"x16" piece of hide. I took it to Chuck and Ferd. They said it had to be chewed. I watched in disbelief as he stuck it in mouth. Ferd chewed on that hide for days till he declared with satisfaction, it was ready. He rolled it and told me how to put it back in and clamp and bolt the jug back on. It went together with a lot more ease than it had come apart. I felt such a magical feeling of accomplishment and astonishment at the same time. I couldn't believe it was actually going back together. We rigged a make-shift pit cock from a model "A" carb filter and a clothes pin. It was hard at first to get it started till I figured out the magneto. Older bikes did not have a battery. The magneto was similar to a pull starter on a lawn mower. As soon as I engaged the magneto the engine roared to life. I felt like electricity was surging along every nerve in my body. The exhilaration of knowing I had succeeded filled my chest till I thought I would explode.

Bubba and I jumped around in circles hollerin at the top of our lungs. I stopped and grabbed Bubba by the shoulders. "It's mine now", I told him. The awe of that realization sunk into our brains for a few brief seconds before we started yellin again. "Why don't we give her a try", Bubba suggested as if the notion was an amazing discovery he had just made. I punched him on the arm and moved an old bucket over to the side of the bike so I could reach and mounted the bike. Bubba slid in behind me. I wasn't exactly sure what to expect but as I released the clutch we took off like a bullet out of a gun. It caught us off guard and I almost lost Bubba but he grabbed on to my shirt. Soon we were soaring up and down the dirt roads of Shanty Town, yelling and waving to everyone we passed. We even rode past Ferd's place and stuck our fists in the air as a salute to the man who made our first flight possible. That night I went to sleep with visions of riding the open roads, strong and free. My life was surely takin a turn for the better. Nothing could stop me now. For a few days Bubba and I had a whole new outlook on life. We attacked our chores with gusto so we could get out on the bike. It was heaven.

One morning I awoke to the sound of my bike's engine. I wiped sleep from

"Sprung From Hell"

my eyes and waited for the fog of sleepiness to blow from my mind. As my thoughts cleared my eyes shot open and my heart missed a beat. There was no reason anyone else should be starting my bike. I jumped from the floor leaving my blanket in a rumpled pile and ran around the front of the house as fast as my little legs would carry me. Just as I rounded the front porch I saw some guy riding away on my bike. I screamed for him to stop and ran a few yards, in desperation, after him but I knew it was no use. I could never catch him and even if I did what was I gonna do? All the weight of my former existence crushed down on me as I watched my freedom ride away. My shoulders bent under the burden of renewed disappointment I turned back toward the house. There stood Uncle Dave, counting out several bills in his hands. I looked at him in disbelief. The betrayal on my face must have been painfully obvious because he almost looked remorseful for a fleeting second. Then quickly regaining his indifferent armor, he shrugged and said, "You'd a killed yourself with that thing". So, he smugly walked away feeling justified that he had only done what was best for me and left me standing small and alone with my shattered dreams crumbled at my feet once again.

A few days later he showed up with a Chief. He promised the same deal. I was still young enough that I believed this was another chance. This time I knew what to look for. It needed a magneto so I took one off a model T in the junk yard. Oddly enough the holes matched up. The T was just a little bigger. I had more fun than I ever had before in my life. Watching the engine come together and knowing it was me that made it work filled a place in my soul that had been empty forever. After I got it working I talked my cousins into lying on the ground in a row so I could jump out a horse shoot over them. They told me I could never make that jump but they still agreed to lie on the ground so I could try. Thankfully I made it and no one got hurt. My uncles were so mad at me though they called my mother to come get me before I killed someone. While waiting for mother to come they sold that bike too.

Even though I had to live with Mother again I would come to stay with Grandmother on the weekends. Bubba and I were spending more time with Ferd and Chuck. Freddie, my cousin, had started hanging around with us too. Chuck had the idea to build a bike of our own from scratch. Well, I had the bike fever now so, I jumped at the idea. Dub Blake was the blacksmith in town and he had an old frame he said I could have. We got the wheels from an old Austin Healey. We pooled all our money and bought an engine from the junk yard for $25.00. It came out of a "53" Chevy. Mr. Blake and Mr. Watts were intrigued by the idea so they did the welding for us. In two days we had built ourselves a "nightmare". It had no tranny so it was either wide open or not at all. We had it set up on blocks. I knew there were some races on a back road behind town and I was determined to enter. Bubba and Freddie were too chicken to ride it. I, on the other hand, couldn't wait to give it a spin. We fired up the engine and I got on. Bubba and Freddie took the blocks off and I took off. I had never felt speed like that before. It was the most exhilarating feeling I had ever experienced. With that kind of power surging under me I was the king of the road.

I headed straight for the race. One thing we had forgotten about was brakes. When I came up on the location for the race I thought of our little oversight. I was tearing down the road and didn't quite know what to do. I steered off the road thinking that the grass would slow me down and be less painful to smash against than the dirt and gravel on the road. It didn't quite work like I planned. I took out two fences and a hen house before I considered I might have to jump. I saw a tree coming straight for me so I bailed. The bike hit the tree head on. It exploded into a thousand pieces. Twisted metal and parts lay scattered all over the ground. I felt sick to my stomach. All that work destroyed in a matter of seconds. People were running up asking if I was okay. As soon as they were assured that I was not seriously injured they started exclaiming about how fast I had been going. "What kind of bike was that?", "Where did you get it?", and "Who did the modifications? Questions flew. I was too stunned at first to answer. Just as I was about to boast that I had done all the work myself, I heard my Mama's voice screaming at an incredible volume. Before I knew what was happening I was being pulled by my ear towards her car. She yelled at me every step of the way and yanked on my ear for emphasis every few words. She resolved that she had to get me away from my uncles before they killed me.

    I never forgot what Ferd and Chuck taught me. I fell in love with motorcycles and that affair is still going on today.

♦ 5 ♦

My Heroes

I DID HAVE A NUMBER OF HEROES who I looked up to in my youth. As a very young boy I liked cowboys. I guess most young boys do. They are strong and confident. No body messes with them. They ride in to town blow away anyone who gets in their way rescue the girl and ride off into the sunset wild and free. Some of my favorites were Tim Holt and Lash Larue. Tim Holt was young and tough. He was the fastest draw in the west. He could draw and shoot and holster his pistol before the bad guy even realized

My Heroes

he had been shot. If I could be like him there would surely be some changes in how people treated me.

Lash Larue was cool because he used an 18' bullwhip. He could make that whip do anything he wanted. It was like it was a snake and he was the snake charmer. He was so handsome all dressed in black there wasn't a lady who could resist him. I made a whip of my own out of old leather shoelaces. I tied them together and braided the long strands into a thick tail. I wrapped another lace around the end to make a handle of sorts. It wasn't exactly like Lash's whip but it made the same sound. Whistling like a blade slashing through the air and exploding with a snap as it made contact with its target. I practiced every day and got really good at hitting what ever I aimed for.

Lash Larue was also the main character in his own comic books. Bubba and I would look through the trash in town and sometimes we would find discarded comic books. They were like treasure. We hid them and guarded them like they were pirate's gold. When we were huddled together in our hiding place going over and over each frame it was like we were actually there. I could hear the sounds of the old western town, the horses and wagons the people milling about, children playing. I could feel the sun and the dust on my skin. The anxious anticipation as Lash appeared on the street ready to face his enemy. The town would suddenly shut down. A hush would descend as children were rushed off the street and doors and windows were banged shut. A woman screamed from somewhere in the distance as the bad guy sauntered out into the open, overconfidently. Mistakenly feeling he had the advantage because he had a gun. Lash looked him square in the eye and

My Heroes

challenged him without saying a word. The bad guy's composer would start to falter. Fear would appear behind his eyes as he realized that Lash wasn't afraid of him or his gun. In desperation he reached for his holster but it was too late. Lash's whip cut through the air like a hot knife through butter and snatched that gun right out of his hand just as if Lash had reached out and taken it from him. But that was not the end of it, quick as a flash he struck again, like lightening, pulling that guy's legs right out from under him. Before he even knew what happened Lash had his hands tied and was handing him off to the Sheriff. The town magically came back to life and the pretty girl ran right into Lash's arms with tears of awe and gratitude streaming down her cheeks. Wow! What I would have given to be Lash Larue.

There were other comic books we would find occasionally. Roy Rogers was one we liked. Trigger and Bullet were great. I think they were smarter than most of the people. But what I really envied about Roy was that he had Dale Evans. She was so pretty and smart and she could ride a horse as good as any man. I loved to hear her sing too. I thought Roy must have been the happiest man alive to have a woman like that who loved him with all her heart. I wondered if anyone would ever love me like that.

Of course there was also Gabby Hayes and Gene Autry and a few others. I spent a lot of time dreaming about being a cowboy. Free to go and do as I pleased. As long as I could have my horse and my gun, or whip, the possibilities were endless. Cowboys remained my heroes till I found out about my Native American ancestry. I could no longer look up to them or respect them because they represented the system that had betrayed and tried to destroy my people.

My Heroes

When I was a little older I found a new hero, James Dean. I saw the movie "Rebel Without a Cause" and it was like I had found a long lost brother. I understood exactly how he felt. The circumstances of the movie and my life were not alike but the emotions associated with Jim's life were so close it thrilled and terrified me at the same time. It was the first time in my life I identified with another human being. Suddenly I was not alone in my existence.

◆ 6 ◆

Last Shred of Innocence Stolen

AT THE AGE OF 8 I STARTED A new life in Oklahoma City. Mother was now living in an apartment building in the big city. It was a 4 story, red brick building pushed up beside a taller structure on a corner in downtown. The dirty windows gazed onto the crowded street like the sad eyes of an old man and the rickety fire escape zigzagged along the side scarring the surface of the bricks.

Last Shred of Innocence Stolen

We lived on the second floor in a 2 room apartment. The living room and dining room and kitchen were all together and there was a separate bedroom with a small bathroom. Mother was still a "working girl". She was what they called a bar fly. She left to go to "work" at about the time most people were heading home. The depressed businessmen and dissatisfied husbands would crowd into the bars to drown their misery and buy a few moments of pleasure. Their loneliness provided my momma's livelihood.

I was once again left to my own devices most of the time. I hung around with a couple of guys in the gang known as the Devils. I liked the sense of family among the members and learned a lot about what brotherhood means from them. But I wasn't ready to trust anyone so, I never joined. I did get into fights almost every day. I think one of the reasons I hung around with the Devils was that it gave me an excuse to fight. I would have found someone to pound on no matter what because the rage inside me had to have a release; the Devils simply provided a steady stream of opportunities.

Mother decided it was not good for me to be left alone. So, she arranged for Betty Jo to watch me. Betty was a retired prostitute who lived on the third floor. I think she must have been pretty at one time. But, when I met her she was a mess. She always wore a faded, satin, night gown with a matching robe. Dirty blonde hair stuck out in several directions at once all over her head and was streaked with gray. She wore makeup but it seemed that she just added more each day without washing off was left from before. Betty introduced me to new drink; wine. I quickly decided I liked this new buzz.

Most days I would come home from school to find Miss Betty flying high. One day when I approached the apartment I could hear music and voices and raucous laughter coming from inside. I opened the door cautiously and peered inside. There were lots of people crowded into the space. Smoke filled the room and mingled with the sweet smell of alcohol. Some people were drinking and talking and laughing. But, as my eyes adjusted to the dim light I saw that several couples were scattered around in various places engaging in sexual acts. I was not shocked at what I saw because I had seen it all before, I was a little taken aback by the fact that they were all doing it in the same room. No one seemed to be ashamed of anything. I came in and closed the door looking for Miss Betty. I wanted to ask if I could have some wine. I maneuvered my way around the people on the floor to the kitchen. Miss Betty was holding a glass of wine with one hand and rubbing the chest of some guy with the other. When she noticed me she leaned down and whispered, "You want a drink little man"? I nodded and reached for the grimy glass she handed me. I turned to go into the den all set to get drunk and watch the party when Miss Betty grabbed my arm. "Where you going sweetie?" she slurred. "To sit on the sofa", I replied. "I have a better idea", she hissed as she pulled me toward the bed room. There were people on the bed but she kicked the mattress and told them to get the hell off her bed. They just moved to the floor and continued as if nothing had happened to interrupt them. She reached for my glass but I drank it in a hurry so she wouldn't take it away. She laughed and patted the bed. I climbed up obediently still not realizing what she had in mind. I had seen adults play the "game" often enough but now it was me. Childhood molestation they call it today.

Last Shred of Innocence Stolen

When Mother found out what had happened she called me a heathen and there was hell to pay. I didn't understand why I was in trouble again. I figured it was my fault, that I somehow caused these things to happen. It didn't matter anyway. I was just a kid and kids don't have any say in what happens. I just knew I was so confused I didn't know how I was supposed to feel. It was like there was dirt and stains all over me that would never go away. I thought everyone could see it on me. I retreated once again deep inside trying to hide to protect myself from their knowing.

My next caretaker was Zelda. She lived on the first floor. Zelda was married, although her husband was rarely there, so Mother must have thought she was more responsible. Mother was not the best judge of character. Zelda preferred Vodka and Gin. When she drank, which was always, she turned mean. She apparently felt that my purpose on this earth was to be her slave. She would sit on her worn out, lumpy sofa drinking and smoking like a chimney, barking out orders to me. I scrubbed her floors on my hands and knees, scoured her bathroom, washed her dishes and picked up her trash. Every day there was something she decided was not clean enough so I had to do it over and over. Once when I had just finished crawling around the kitchen floor with a scrub brush for over an hour, she came stumbling in and knocked the trash can over onto the floor. She screamed at me, "Now look what you've made me do"! She slapped me across the face with the back of her hand so hard my lip busted open and my cheek swelled. "Clean up your mess and scrub the damn floor again ", she railed. I could feel heat rising up from my chest to my neck like steam pressure fixin to spew from my ears. If I could have I'd have killed her right there. The fact that I was too little to do it only infuriated me more. The fear of what she would do to me was greater than my need for revenge at that time though, so I started picking up the trash.

A few days later I came to Zelda's after school to find her completely wasted. She must have been drinking all day long. There were crumpled tissues all over the table and floor. Zelda sat with her head in her hands. When she heard me come in she looked up and I could see she had been crying. Her nose was raw and shiny and her swollen eyes were rimmed with red. She sniffed and demanded to know what had taken me so long to get home from school. I had arrived at the same time I did every day, but didn't see the point in arguing. It would only set her off. I shrugged and said, "I guess I just walked slower than usual". I saw a momentary surge of anger flash behind her eyes, but it passed and her eyes began to well with fresh tears. Then she looked at me as if she was pleading with me to understand her pain.

This was something I had never dealt with before. It scared me to death. Something inside me screamed," run"! But my legs were rooted to the floor. She pulled me toward her and held onto my arms. I could smell the gin and feel her hot breath on my face. I braced myself for the blow I knew was coming, but instead she started stroking my hair. I was completely taken off guard. I looked at her face and asked sheepishly, "are you okay"? She smiled a funny, sick smile and leaned back in her chair releasing my arm. "Sit down and have a drink with me", she offered. I wasn't about to pass up an offer to drink, so I sat in the chair across from her. She poured some gin in the dirty glass in front of her and handed it to me. I relished the familiar feel of it burning down my throat. I started to relax. That was my first mistake.

She waited till I had finished my drink and poured me another. She watched me sip from the glass for a few seconds before she asked what had happened with Betty and why my mother took me away from her. Beginning to feel the effect of the gin, I made my second mistake. I told her everything. I saw a longing wash across her face. The alarms started going off in my head. "Finish your drink", she instructed. I tipped the glass and drained it. I wasn't sure what was coming, but I knew, whatever it was, I'd rather be drunk than sober for it. She pulled me down from the chair and over to face her again. She held tight to one of my arms as she unbuttoned her blouse with the other. She gave me instructions as to what she wanted me to do. I felt bile rising in my throat at the awareness that the "games" were about to begin again.

"Sprung From Hell"

So, my after school "duties" took on a whole new meaning. I was now Zelda's distraction from the uselessness of her life. She made me do things I had never seen or heard of. If it wasn't done to her satisfaction I got a beating. She also took to burning me with cigarettes or a curling iron or clothes iron or whatever. She seemed to take pleasure in seeing my agony. Like inflicting pain on me somehow relieved her's.

On one of my trips to Grandmother's she noticed the burn marks on one of my arms. She demanded to know what had caused them. I wasn't about to lie to her. She had a direct line to God and she surely would tell him to send me straight to hell and I was sure He would comply. So, I spilled my story. She clamped her hand over her mouth and wailed like someone had just died. I stood transfixed, watching her mourn; what I did not know. "Oh! God, why have you given me this heathen child? Purge the wickedness from his soul!" she groaned. It seemed an eternity before she stopped. When she looked down at me I swear I could see the fires of hell burning in her eyes. "You will stay in the cellar until God decides to forgive you", she proclaimed with her arm stretched out pointing me to my sinner's prison. I marched in front of her out the door to the cellar with my head down and tears stinging my eyes. I would not look up, for I wasn't about to let anyone see me crying.

During my time of penance I had time to think about my life. I came to the conclusion that I was going to hell in a hand basket. There was no hope for me. No matter what I did or didn't do I was marked as a heathen. I felt I had no chance in life. My mother didn't want me, my father didn't care one way or the other about me, I was an embarrassment to Grandmother and the rest of the family, a burden and problem nobody wanted. The belief that I was forever to be a worthless, half-wit, heathen burned deep into my soul. The scars of that branding remain today.

My hell was not over when I was released from the cellar. The report of my sins had spread through the family. Apparently when Ross and Dave and my other uncles were drunk at the still it wasn't just girls who came to play. They decided it was time for me to join the "fun". Uncle Dave was first. He brought some Red Eye for us to share. He asked me about Betty and Zelda. The Red Eye loosened my tongue and I began to tell all that had gone on. Before long Dave had unzipped his trousers and was getting his jollies while listening to me talk of my experiences. When I stopped talking, staring at him in disbelief, he handed me the bottle and said, "Get on with it". I took a good, long swig from the bottle and continued my tale. He asked for more details than I cared to share, but he was insistent. Next thing I knew he had my pants unzipped and was masturbating me. This confused me more than I had ever been confused before. I began to question whether or not I was a normal guy. Things went down hill from there. Uncle Ross, who not only drank but used heroine as well, got in on it. He sodomized me. It was degrading and dehumanizing. I was sure now that I must not be right. I wondered if I was what they called a homo. That fear plagued me for years.

I could never tell Grandmother. My shame was complete, my young life a shambles and there was no hope of deliverance on the horizon. I was already in hell. But change was on the horizon I was about to enter a strange new world that would change my life forever.

◆ 7 ◆

Rescued

BY THIS TIME I REALLY HAD THE idea of running away but I wasn't too sure where to run to. I thought about death being an escape route but I wasn't clear how to go about that either. I knew the Bible didn't present a pretty picture of the destination of heathens but I didn't really care. I looked at life as trouble and I was the cause. I drank most every day and into the night. I hated myself and my life. Alcohol seemed the only avenue for temporary escape. In the midst of my

Rescued

hopelessness an unexpected passageway opened up.

I was nine and had been sent to the cellar once again. Dreading another visit from one of my uncles I crouched behind a barrel in the corner. I knew hiding would not work for long but maybe it could postpone the inevitable. I heard the hinges on the heavy door begin to creak. I cringed and tried to shrink into the corner, fear and disgust churning in my stomach.

The old wooden door groaned in protest as it was opened slowly, almost cautiously. That was strange. My uncles were always drunk and would throw the door open carelessly. Someone was creeping down the stairs. He was much smaller than either of my uncles. Maybe he was a thief coming to steal some of our food. Well, let him! I certainly didn't care. I peered curiously around the belly of the barrel. He stopped at the bottom of the stairs and squinted into the darkness. "I know you're in here", he whispered loudly. "I watched em put you in". Who was he and why was he watching me? I remained hidden not sure what he intended to do. "Will you just come out, we gotta git", he stated urgently. I thought he wanted me to come out and play with him or something. Was he crazy! It was well after dark. Besides if I left the cellar without permission I would get the strap for sure. Then it hit me, I had never had the opportunity to leave the cellar before. I was always locked in from the outside. Suddenly the prospect of escaping my prison cell before my uncles came to call seemed to be my salvation. This young stranger was an angel sent to deliver me or a demon to lure me into bigger trouble than I was already in, but I didn't care it was a chance and I had to take it. I stepped out of my hiding place and stood looking at this apparition who was my deliverer. He looked human enough. "Let's go, we gotta get outta here now", he urged waving me toward the stairs. I just followed without uttering a word wondering if he was about to lead me to hell.

We ran across the street and ducked behind an old car. He scanned the distance we had just crossed and watched the front of my house for a few seconds. I guess everything checked out okay because he motioned me to follow him again. We passed several shacks then turned up the path that led to a house standing back from the road a ways. There was a man and a lady and a girl a little older than me standing beside a truck with some boxes and suitcases in the back. "That's my boy", the man said pounding my ghost friend on the shoulder. He smiled down at me and said, "Get in the back of the truck boy; I'm taking you out of hell". As if I was being controlled by some outside force my legs started moving towards the truck. I don't think I meant for them to but they kept going, climbing obediently over the tailgate and kneeling in the back. The ghost hopped effortlessly in beside me and looked sideways at me like I had just sprouted horns. "It's gonna be okay", he assured me with a pat on my shoulder.

I soon accepted the fact that my angel of deliverance was in fact just a guy. His name was Jonny and he was about six or seven years older than me. The man was his father and the girl was his sister Carol. The lady's name was Lauren, I don't think she was their mother but it didn't matter. His father had somehow found out about what was going on with me and he didn't like it. He took matters into his own hands and decided to take me to California with him and his family.

So, there I was on my way to a place I had never heard of with people I didn't know. Speeding down the open highway in the back of a pickup truck with humid wind whipping my hair into my face, I looked up at the stars sparkling like diamonds on a backdrop of black velvet and wondered if I was dreaming. Jonny slugged me on the arm and motioned for me to sit down. No, I wasn't dreaming, I definitely felt that slug. Jonny was not really very big but he was solid muscle. We drove for what seemed to me like an eternity. We would stop along the way to eat and sleep, camping out under the stars. Jonny and I would sleep in the bed of the truck. The weather was mild and comfortable. I was used to sleeping on the ground so the truck bed suited me just fine. It was pretty luxurious actually with the thick sleeping bag Lauren gave me to wrap up in. After a while the terror and excitement that had been swirling around in my head started to settle down and I relaxed a little. Jonny and I became good friends over the next several days. He told me we were going to a place called California that was near the ocean. He had lived there all his life and stated matter-of-factly that it was the best place in the world to live. We would be staying with some friends of theirs till his dad got them a place.

Mr. B. liked to drink beer and have a good time but he was never anything but nice to me. He told me I would never have to live in hell again. He and Jonny were more like buddies than father and son. Carol was a motherly type who doted on Jonny and her father. They took it good-naturedly though I could tell it annoyed Jonny sometimes. They were obviously very close to each other. Lauren was a nice lady too. I secretly relished the feeling of being cared for. I tried to savor every little kindness because I knew it couldn't last. As soon as they figured out that I was a half-wit, hellion they would probably just leave me on the side of the road. But, for the moment, it was amazing.

When we arrived in California it was like landing on a different planet. The sky was a brilliant blue and trees never looked so green or so tall. Everything seemed to be bathed in sunshine. We drove to a neighborhood near Oakland with modest homes lining the paved street. They each had a small yard in the front carpeted with lush green grass and accented with occasional splashes of bright colored flowers. The houses themselves were painted in soft, muted colors that reflected the light from the sun so that they almost glowed. I was blown away.

The greatest thing was there were bikes parked in almost every driveway or in the street out in front of the houses. I must have had my mouth hanging open because Jonny slugged me in the arm again and said, "close your mouth before

"Sprung From Hell"

you catch a fly". I rubbed my arm where he had punched me and just continued to stare in amazement.

We pulled into one of the driveways and Mr. B. cut the engine. He blasted the horn a couple of times and got out of the truck. The front door opened and I watched the biggest man I had ever laid eyes on emerge from the house. I thought he must have been a monster. Roy was easily over six feet tall and his chest was as wide as one of the barrels in the cellar. His head was covered in thick auburn hair that hung to his shoulders and an equally thick beard sprouted from his chin. A huge grin was spread across his face as he heartily greeted and hugged his friends. Following him from the house was a petite, young woman with long, straight, light brown hair and an inviting smile. She too embraced each member of the family. She turned and noticed me climbing out of the truck. "Who is

Rescued

this?" she asked. I shrank back slightly as the possibility of rejection raised its ugly head once again. Jonny slung his arm around my shoulders and said, "We found him on the side of the road and thought he looked so pitiful we should pick him up, so we did". Soft laughter bubbled to the surface as she leaned down slightly to honor me with a hug. "Welcome to the family", she said. Those four simple words soaked into my heart like long awaited rain on parched soil. They held more meaning for me than anyone could have possibly known. Delia moved into a special place in my heart at that very moment.

Roy rode a Triumph, sometimes called a Trumpet. He spent a lot of time working on his bike and the bikes of his friends. Roy was amazed at how much I knew about engines. I told him about the bikes I had worked on. He made me his official "wrench boy". I hung around Roy and his friends as much as I could. They were rough and crude but they accepted me as a part of their group. I finally felt like I belonged and not only belonged but was actually wanted. Roy said I was a better motorcycle mechanic than most of his buddies.

Roy and Delia had two younger kids, Nathan and Stacy. Delia took up being a mother to me. I guess it just sorta came natural to her since she already had two kids it was easy to add one more. I tried my best to be good so they wouldn't have any reason to send me away.

About three or four weeks after we arrived Mr. B. found a place for him and his family. They moved a few miles away. Roy and Delia asked me if I would like to stay with them. You bet I would! I couldn't believe my good fortune. Nobody had ever wanted me to stay with them. I was always a burden people were trying to pass off to someone else. Tears of sheer elation and overwhelming gratitude stung at my eyes and threatened to spill over. I swallowed the lump in my throat and held them at bay. I wanted to show Roy that I was a man and men didn't cry. All I could do was nod my head with enthusiasm. Roy mussed up my hair and simply said, "Good, I need you to help me with the bikes". We bid farewell to Mr. B. and the rest of the gang. They weren't going far and we would still see them often. I was starting to see what a family really was.

Shortly after Jonny moved away Delia's nephew came to live with us. They called him Mums, as in the saying "Mum's the word", because his daddy had cut out his tongue when he was little because he wouldn't stop crying. As a result he couldn't speak very well. He was about three years older than me and we became best friends. He taught me how to communicate with my hands so when he tried to tell me something I couldn't understand he could sign it to me. We got really good at understanding one another. Mums loved bikes like me and we enjoyed working on them together. The other kids were littler than us so we didn't spend much time hanging around with them.

Jonny was in school but he also worked at a bike shop. Mums and I would hang out with him as often as we could. I was never happier than when I was working on a bike. I learned every detail of what made an engine run smoothly. I knew every bolt and screw by heart. No matter who was broke down or what the problem was we could fix it. The shop was my favorite place on earth. I loved everything about it, the smell of oil and gasoline, the sounds of tools banging around creating a sort-of off beat symphony mingled with the loud rock music pumping from the radio and the colorful conversations of the mechanics bound to each other in a brotherhood of hard work and fast bikes. Mums and I were a part of that brotherhood; we were the kid brothers, but still brothers none-the-less.

Roy had a reputation as the best bike mechanic around. He also rode with a club. I don't know for sure what they were called. The club members wore a vest with a patch sewn on the back signifying what club they were associated with. The patch had several pieces to it and each one had to be earned. In order to become what was known as a full patch member a prospective candidate had to go through a time of initiation. During this time, which varied from person to person, they were referred to as a prospect. Once a man had earned his full patch he was not only a member, but a brother.

A young man named Wiley was a prospect who helped out at the shop.

"Sprung From Hell"

Sometimes the members can be hard on a prospect. He has to do whatever the members ask of him. They enjoy making a prospect work his butt off. Wiley liked having me and Mums around to help him do whatever tedious, exhausting job they tasked him with. We didn't mind, we just wanted to be there.

There were days that we stayed home. See, Delia was a great lady but she wasn't perfect. Delia was not her real name; I don't know what her real name was. She was called Delia because of the pills she often took. Most of the time she was fine, but every so often she would take too much and just crash on the couch. On those days Mums and I would stay home to take care of her and watch out for the younger kids. We owed her that much at least.

Well, fixin bikes was not the only thing I learned during my stay in California. I learned to be a man. Roy and

Jonny were my instructors and they were tough. This particular phase of my education would prove to be very instrumental in the course my life would take.

◆ 8 ◆

Life Lessons Learned

ALTHOUGH I HAD BEEN IN MY share of fights and had won a number of them I was not skilled. Mums and I had a disagreement one day that came to blows. Mums landed a solid punch to my jaw. I ran into the house complaining that He had hurt me. Roy looked at me and said, "What are you whining about"? "He hurt me", I whimpered. "Boy, you don't know how to fight do you"? I stared at the floor and just shook my head. "Lessons start now", he announced, grabbing me by the shirt sleeve and pulling me toward

Life Lessons Learned

the back yard. Once outside he yelled for Mums to come help him. I looked pleadingly at Mums not knowing what was about to take place. "I'm teaching Kenner how to protect himself and you're his sparring partner", Roy explained. Mums looked at me with a big, stupid grin on his face and signed, "This will be fun". I felt like a puppy at the mercy of a couple of mischievous kids.

Lessons became an every day event. Jonny would join in on my training most days. I caught on quickly. Soon I was giving Mums a whipping. I learned how to block and how to land a strategically placed punch that would do the most damage with the least amount of effort. I learned that I could use my legs, knees, elbows and head as well as my fists. They also taught me to use things that were within my reach as weapons if necessary.

All of the lessons I learned were not physical. They began to counter some of the lies I had been told all my life. They said I was not a worthless half-wit, I was smart and a fast learner. They said I did not have to be the person others wanted me to be even if they were my relatives. I could be my own man. I didn't have to let anyone hurt me again. I also began to learn what brotherhood was all about. We stand up for each other no matter what. A brother is a brother and nothing can change that. Family was a concept I was finally beginning to grasp.

I was soon given an opportunity to use my new skills. A neighbor kid said something ugly about Delia. It made my blood boil till I could almost feel the steam escaping from my ears. The old familiar rage rose up inside me. For a split second I forgot everything I had recently learned. I lunged at him and I left my guard down. He caught me on the side of the head. Little lights exploded in my brain and I felt myself going down but

Life Lessons Learned

I was helpless to stop it. The other guys stood over me laughing at my demise. Old wounds were reopened so as soon as the fireworks in my head stopped I picked myself up and ran home.

Roy, Jonny and Skull were in the kitchen with some of the other guys. Jonny grabbed my arm and wouldn't let me pass. I tried to avoid looking him in the face because he would know right away that I had been crying. He twisted my arm till I had to look at him. "Did you forget everything we taught you, boy?" He demanded. I couldn't find my voice, but about that time Mums walked in. Jonny got the full story from him.

Roy stood to his full height and slammed his massive fist into the palm of his other hand while stating that this was the end of this foolishness. They all marched me down the street to the house where this kid lived. His father answered the door and he and Roy spoke briefly.

"Sprung From Hell"

His dad yelled into the house for his son to come out. The next thing I knew me and him were facing each other with all the men standing in a circle around us. Jonny said, "You beat his ass or I'll beat yours". I knew he meant it too. As I looked into his face I resolved that this was the day I would transition from childhood to manhood. This was my independence day. Every beating, every abuse, every cruel word I had ever endured flashed through my mind. I narrowed my eyes and pressed my lips together in determination. All this took place in a split second. I lunged at him with all the fury that the years of pain had trapped inside me. But this time I was focused. It didn't matter if I made it out alive or not. I was going to maintain control and prove myself a man if I died trying.

I'm not sure how long we were pounding on each other because time lost all meaning. I felt every blow on my face and body but I was oblivious to the pain. I could taste blood in my mouth and feel sweat stinging my eyes but I just kept swinging. After a while I heard Roy say, "Enough". Jonny wrapped his arms around my chest and pulled me back, away from the kid. I struggled against him for a few seconds. He held tight till I settled down. The intensity of the moment drained from my body and I slumped against Jonny "You did good, little man, I'm proud of you", he said. I straightened up and turned to look Jonny in the eye. I saw encouragement there with just a touch of sadness. I wondered if this new world of manhood might be a tougher place to live than I realized at that moment. No matter, I was a man now and I wasn't ever going back.

Then I remembered the other guy. I turned to see him sitting on the ground with his dad leaning over him saying something. I wondered if he was feeling the same as me. He looked pretty bloody and bruised. Based on how my face was throbbing and my lip was beginning to swell, I figured I must look just as bad. I swiped at my stinging eyes and was shocked to see blood, not sweat, on my hand as I brought it down. The bright red smear was like a badge I had earned and it felt good.

Roy declared the fight a tie and made us shake hands. He instructed us that this ended our disagreement and we were to treat each other as family from now on. I offered him my hand and he reached to accept it. We each looked through swollen eyes at our puffy, purplish faces and we started to chuckle. Soon the entire group was overcome with laughter. Two boys had shown themselves to be worthy of the title, "Man", and the bonds of brotherhood had been preserved. It was a good day.

Life Lessons Learned

Jonny and Roy continued to work with me every day. I acquired new skills and learned new techniques and grew stronger by the day. I knew that I would never allow anyone to hurt me again.

The next lesson came on one of the best days of my life. It was my 10th birthday. I awoke that day to the aroma of a baking cake. I followed the enticing scent to the kitchen and found Delia standing at the counter carefully frosting a chocolate cake with fluffy white icing. She glanced up at me as I entered the room and flashed me a lovely smile. "Happy birthday, sleepy head", she beamed. I couldn't believe my eyes or my ears. I stared at her with my mouth gaping open. "What's a matter with you? Haven't you ever seen a birthday cake before?" she joked.

A lump formed in my throat and my bottom lip started to quiver. I willed it to be still but the harder I tried the more it rebelled. The truth was, I had only seen pictures of birthday cakes. I knew they existed, but I thought they were only for rich kids and certainly not for the likes of me. My brain could not seem to wrap itself around this new experience. How did she even know it was my birthday? Why did she care? Why would she go to the trouble of baking me a cake? Did I deserve such special treatment? Wow! It sure felt good. I blinked a couple times and shook my head. My mouth still could not form words so I just looked at her. I knew she understood. A soft sadness clouded her features and misted her eyes for a fleeting moment.

Then just as suddenly as the cloud came, it blew away. She was once again fun-loving Delia. She extended both hands toward the counter, like a magician's assistant to showcase the cake and said, "Ta Da…" It looked like a cake from a cartoon, a little lopsided, leaning

Life Lessons Learned

precariously off the edge of the plate. It was covered in so much fluff it appeared it might have floated away with the slightest breeze. She had carefully poked 11 small, colored candles into the fluff. It was the most beautiful cake in the whole world. I smiled the biggest smile I could muster, till it hurt my cheeks, and it still wasn't big enough to show how happy I was. She playfully slugged me on the arm and told me to go get dressed because the family would be showin up soon. I floated, not walked, down the hall.

Before long there were people everywhere. Everyone was having fun. I had just experienced, for the first time, standing in the center of a circle of people who were not making fun of me or hurting me, but singing to me! They all cheered as I blew out the candles. "What did you wish for?" Jonny wanted to know. I shrugged my shoulders and said, "I didn't know I was supposed to make a wish". "What!" he exclaimed, "Light the candles again". I wished that this day could last forever, even though I knew that was impossible.

I was still floating as Delia served pieces of the cake, with ice cream! All the men were standing around in the front-yard and the women were sitting in the living room. We kids were enjoying our cake and ice cream in the kitchen. Suddenly a sound so loud it seemed to crack the very air around us exploded somewhere outside. Some of the women screamed and they all jumped up from their seats looking at each other with panic and confusion. Mums and I looked at each other and came to the same immediate conclusion. Something cool was happening and we better go see what it was before the ladies came to their senses and made us stay inside. We jumped up and ran out the back door just as Delia and another mom entered the kitchen.

Life Lessons Learned

We rounded the corner of the house and saw the men crowded around a truck in the street. The truck took off with tires screeching. Roy and Jonny and the other guys were talking and gesturing wildly. I could tell something was wrong. I looked at Mums and he signed that the sound we had heard was a gun shot. I surveyed the yard and the group of men till I was satisfied that no one I cared about had been hurt.

Just then Delia walked cautiously out onto the front lawn. Her eyes sought frantically for Roy. When their eyes locked I saw a flood of relief rush over her. She waited for Roy to give her the okay with a nod of his head and she ran to him. He enfolded her in a protective embrace and stroked her hair. She leaned her head back to look at him and I could read his lips as he told her everything was under control. She turned to go back inside and report to the other ladies.

Mums and I ran to intercept her. "What happened?" I asked. She patted my head like a little kid and said, "Nothing, don't worry about it". I was irritated and a little hurt that she didn't think I was grown-up enough to know what was going on.

I turned to Mums to see if he was as irritated as me. He had a kind of sympathetic look on his face. I felt like punching him right in the nose. "So, what do you know that I don't?" I asked accusingly. "It was a drug deal gone bad", he stated matter-of-factly. I looked across the yard and pointed at Jonny, "Was he in it?" I inquired. Mums didn't answer he just turned and walked away. Mums was learning and I wasn't.

I was too consumed with conflicting thoughts and emotions to be angry with him at that moment. I wanted to be a part of the adult world and be included among the men, but I had just enjoyed my very first birthday party as a kid. Lesson number 2; being a kid has its advantages. I decided I would keep my eyes open and learn as much as I could. When the day came for me to be accepted among their ranks, I'd be ready.

♦ 9 ♦

Biker World

BIKES WERE THE ONE THING that always remained constant. I learned more every day about the biker culture and way of life.

As far back as World War I the military used bike riders as couriers, scouts and dispatchers. The Harley Davidson Company manufactured thousands of bikes for the government during the 1930's and 1940's. Hitler took it even further with his war machine actually mounting machine guns on BMW bikes and using them in combat.

As a result, men coming home from the war brought with them a restless, kick ass attitude that was represented by riding full speed, unafraid on a powerful bike. These men had come from hell and found it difficult to settle into a quiet, suburban, white picket fence life. Many of them formed brotherhoods. Some say this was the beginning of "Outlaw Motorcycle Clubs". Most clubs started with good ideas about family and standing together against life's trials. They wanted to ride the open road and enjoy the freedom they had fought for in the war.

Roy and Jonny and the others were riders with one of these groups. Sometime after my 10th birthday I witnessed my first caravan. The brothers were going camping. It was known as a "Rally". Delia took me and Mums in the truck ahead of the bikes. There were 3 other trucks and 2 cars driven by other "old ladies". We were to set up camp so it would be ready when all the riders showed up.

At first there were about 100 bikes. Soon they met up with another chapter and by the time we were out of town another group had joined us. Man! What a sight that was. I stared in utter awe from the back of the truck. All you could see, for miles and miles were motorcycles. Like a giant snake winding its way along the country side. I could feel the rumble of 100s of engines like thunder coming from under ground. I will never forget that feeling. Something historic and monumental was taking place, to my way of thinking, and I was a part of it.

After we set up camp and had a Bar-B-Q it was time for the young ones to head to bed. There was a separate area set up that was designated for the "Party". We children weren't allowed to leave camp. We could hear it though. I dreamed of the day I would be a part of that world.

After a couple of days of hanging out, partying and having a good time we had to load up and head home. One of the members of another group, named Madman, broke down on the ride back. He was a monster of a man, made Roy look like a baby. He was probably 6'7" tall and weighed about 300 lbs. He had broken a chain. I had never seen anyone break a link and not to have to buy a new chain. I offered to help and he showed me how to make a clip lock out of a hair pin. He called it "nigger riggin" it. I couldn't believe it worked, but it did. That term became a part of my vocabulary and stuck with me a long time till I found out it was considered derogatory.

Another brother slung a piston. There was nothing that could be done about that. We hauled it in the back of the truck. The trip home turned into a long ordeal because everyone was breaking down. The bike in the truck became a parts bike. I remember thinking, "I'm glad it's not mine". We finally made it back and life settled into a routine.

Jonny found it difficult to be content in a regular job environment. He wasn't cut out for a mediocre existence. He decided to join the military. He was too young, so he forged his birth certificate and entered the Army. It didn't take long for them to figure out what he had done. Because of a recent change in the regulations he scored an honorable discharge and returned to California.

He and some of his buddies formed a group. They needed a name and a patch. One of the riders, named Cowboy, had an old air force patch he had found. Jonny thought it was cool so they adopted it and the name associated with it. The bottom rocker read "Sacto". The rocker is an embroidered strip, sometimes crescent shaped, that goes below the patch to identify the city in which a club's chapter is based. Instead of putting "Oakland "on their patches they settled on being "Nomads".

There were 13 original guys in this outlaw group. Jonny was an analytical thinker and liked things to be run in a disciplined fashion. Cowboy was appointed to be the first president of their club. The other members didn't seem to place the same significance on discipline and order that Jonny did. He spent a lot of time being frustrated with their lack of organization. He spent every waking hour consumed with thoughts of how to whip this little group into something formidable.

As fate would have it, Jonny and one other brother took off on a ride to Southern California late in the summer. Jonny's transmission chose this time to break down. Out of nowhere a guy pulls up on a bike asking if he can help. Jonny noticed right away that he was wearing a patch just like theirs. When Jonny and Cowboy had chosen that emblem and name they had no idea that another club by that name already existed.

This guy's name was, Hic. He took them to the clubhouse and introduced them to the members who were hanging out. They were really cool guys. They helped get Jonny's bike back on the road. They put them up for a couple of days while waiting for the bike to be fixed and Hic gave Jonny the scoop on how a motorcycle club should be run. He told him about dues, meetings, rules, organization and officers. It was a lot like the military and this appealed to Jonny.

He returned to Oakland with the plan of becoming the first Oakland chapter of this outlaw club. A few weeks later two officers from the So-Cal chapter came to visit and it was made official. Technically the Oakland chapter was "illegal" because they were never voted in, but that doesn't matter now.

Shortly after they became official, Cowboy left to pursue a career in music. Jonny became the president of the Oakland chapter at the age of 18.

In 1948 there was an event that has been labeled the "Hollister Incident". What started out to be a sanctioned American Motorcyclist Association racing competition went downhill when some riders from several outlaw clubs got drunk and out of hand, many of them were arrested. This was a severe blow to the AMA's credibility. They released an official statement claiming that only one percent of motorcycle riders were the outlaw clubs that gave bike riding a bad name, the other ninety-nine percent were good, law abiding citizens.

Not long after Jonny became president there was another AMA sanctioned event with over 3700 riders in attendance. Two members of one of the outlaw clubs were involved in a very ugly accident and were killed. The AMA decided to cancel all future events.

All the clubs from Southern California and the Bay Area held a meeting. They were tired of the AMA's propaganda. They adopted the name that the AMA had forced on them and wore it proudly. The "One-Percenters" became a sign of prestige in the biker world. A patch was designed. It was a triangle with a 1% symbol inside it. Jonny's club was one of the ones that wore that symbol.

The brotherhood among the club members was taken very seriously. If you messed with one you messed with all. I saw the vengeance of the club first-hand when a brother was beat to death by the police in a small town in California. The club rode out as one huge entourage bent on finding the man responsible

Biker World

and making him pay. Delia said we had to go. "You boys stay close to me", she instructed. We parked about 4 or 5 blocks outside of town. There was one main street running down the center of the town, it was probably called Main St. but I really don't know. It wasn't a long street; there were only two stop lights. Along either side there were little shops with quaint window dressings. There was a bakery, a butcher, a post office and of course, the police department. That was where the club headed. From our position we could hear the rumble of the bike engines heralding the arrival of judgment. They never started off wanting to hurt anyone but the guy who had killed their brother, but when an outlaw club is on the war-path you don't want to be in their way.

For hours, late into the night, we could hear motorcycles racing up and down the street, glass breaking, and people screaming. It felt surreal, like we had entered another world. My mind created images to go along with the sounds surrounding me. However, none of the things I imagined prepared me for what I would see the next morning.

Mums and I had fallen asleep in the bed of the truck sometime during the night. We awoke to an eerie quiet as the sun rose slowly shedding soft light on the road that led into town. We could tell Delia was nervous. She was pacing along the side of the truck, back and forth; back and forth. I don't think she ever went to sleep. It's a wonder there wasn't a groove in the pavement where she was pacing. As dawn broke she resolved to go into town to see for herself what was going on. She knew Roy would be angry but her fear that something had happened to him was greater than her fear of his anger. She slowly drove the truck closer to the edge of town and pulled over in front of a small house. She cautioned us to stay in the truck and walked resolutely down the sidewalk.

I looked at Mums and he knew right away I had no intention of staying in the truck. He nodded at me in silent agreement. As soon as Delia was out of sight we jumped down and followed the same sidewalk she had taken but we ducked periodically behind parked vehicles and trash cans to make sure we would not been seen. After about two blocks we began to see signs of what had transpired in the night. The manicured front lawns of the houses close to downtown were shredded and torn by the deep gouges left from spinning tires. Windows of houses as well as cars were shattered and glass shards littered the ground. The closer we came to the center of town the worse it got. The air was sharp with the smell of burning rubber. A car in the middle of an intersection was engulfed

"Sprung From Hell"

in flames and billows of tar black smoke boiled up to the sky. I recognized a few of the brothers. Some were sprawled on a patch of grass in front of the post office as if they were lounging in a park. A few others were going through the contents of a car perched oddly on top of a bench with two wheels in the air. I could hear crying coming from somewhere inside one of the shops. It was then that I noticed there were people lying in the street and on the sidewalk. Some were moving, some were not, but they were all beaten pretty badly. Blood was splattered over the ground and the fronts of the stores. As I surveyed the scene I was not overcome with grief or even pity. I felt an odd sense of justice and power. At that moment my conscience was seared. I felt no remorse. I was excited by what I saw. In power there was protection and the Outlaw lifestyle would provide me with power. I found out later that the cop who had killed our brother confessed and was dealt with accordingly. The club made its own judgments and exacted its own vengeance. Only those who tried to interfere got hurt. I was proud to be associated with this way of life.

I let my eyes roam over the destruction feeling satisfied that this was justice. My eye caught sight of a familiar bike over on its side in front of the grocery. Jonny's colors were on the ground too. I sprinted to the fallen bike as if I had to save it and the colors from humiliation. I reverently lifted the vest from the ground and dusted it off. I hefted the bike to an upright position. That was when it occurred to me to put the vest on and sit on the bike. I just wanted to dream of what it would be like someday when I was a full patch member.

I hadn't noticed that several news stations had arrived. How they got wind of what had happened, even before any other law enforcement had shown up, I'll never know. I sat straight and tall on Jonny's bike as flash bulbs started popping all around me. Jonny and some others heard the commotion and came rushing out onto the sidewalk. When he saw me on his bike wearing his colors he stopped short and just stared at me. For a split second I thought I was as good as dead. But he burst into laughter and said, "You think you're hot shit, don't you kid"? So, there, in the middle of mayhem, the brothers shared a moment of laughter and camaraderie.

It was short lived, however. Sirens wailed in the distance. Jonny waived his arm in the air in a circular motion as a signal that it was time to ride out. "Give me my colors kid and get back to the truck", he commanded. As I started off toward the street where we had left the truck parked he hollered after me, "Your day will come". I dreamed of that day as I rushed down the street.

Little did I know that one of those photographs that I had posed for so proudly would be published in the Saturday Evening Post, on the front page, with the headline reading, "Youngest Gang Member". That is how my family found me.

♦ 10 ♦

No Longer a Victim

ABOUT A MONTH AND A HALF later I awoke to voices in the front room. One of those voices sounded very familiar. It took me back to a place I didn't want to go. Panic seized my heart as I realized, that was my mama's voice. My first thought was to hide, but where? I could run away. I could go out the window and just keep running, but I knew that was a dumb idea, because I had no place to go. They would find me anyway. I was trapped. Hopelessness and despair crept into my very soul and wrapped around my heart. Suddenly my whole body seemed to be made of lead. I was too heavy to move. I just sank into the mattress and waited for the inevitable.

It wasn't long till Mama and Delia came into the room. As soon as Mama saw me she ran over to the bed and threw her arms around me as if she had been agonizing over my absence. I just sat like a lump on a log. There was no warmth in her embrace. I knew this was a show for Delia's benefit. I looked over Mama's shoulder at Delia, standing in the doorway, my eyes pleading with her not to be fooled by this charade. I saw so many conflicting emotions waging a battle behind her eyes. Mama said, "I've come to take you home". The heaviness affected my tongue so that I was unable to protest, although I wanted to scream with all my might. Delia began moving silently around the room gathering my few belongings into a grocery bag. She placed some clean clothes on the end of the bed for me to change into and walked slowly out the door. "I'll be waitin in the front room for you darlin", mama said with a too sweet smile.

Like a robot on automatic pilot I moved mechanically around the room, getting dressed, retrieving some treasures I'd hidden, and pulling on my shoes. The thought occurred to me that these were the first shoes I ever had that fit right and didn't hurt my feet. I looked around the room and felt the same comfortable feeling I got from the shoes. Inside me a small boy wailed and screamed, "Nooooo…". On the outside, a young man and future member of an outlaw motorcycle club, stood tall and ready to face whatever was coming.

Delia and Mother were talking in the living room when I entered grocery bag in hand. They continued for several minutes till Mother noticed me. She walked over to where I stood and looked me up and down. "My you've gotten tall", she commented as if she was just then coming to the realization that I had changed and she really didn't have a clue how much. Then her plastic smile returned and she hugged me awkwardly, patting me on the back as she promised things would be different from now on.

We walked out to a yellow, checkered cab waiting in the street. Delia held on to me for a long time. She could no longer hold back the pain and frustration. Her petite frame shook with sobs as I embraced her. "She has a court order, there's nothing we can do, we tried", she explained in broken syllables through her tears. "You know you always have a place where you're welcome". It made sense now. "I know, it's alright", I soothed her even though inside I was wailing. Mother was standing beside the cab tapping her foot impatiently and finally said, "We need to go or we'll miss the bus". Delia reluctantly let go of me and looked into my eyes. I knew she was aware of my fear and pain and that only caused me to hurt more. I turned and walked on wooden legs into an uncertain and frightening future. Mother climbed into the cab after me and slammed the door. I watched out the back window as Delia got smaller and imagined myself being sucked into a black abyss. She waved until I couldn't see her anymore. I settled into the seat and realized I didn't get to say goodbye to Mums.

We pulled into the bus station just in time to board the bus headed to Oklahoma. Once we were seated in the bus Mother's tune changed. She glared at me and twisted her fingers in my long hair. She pulled hard and steady as she commanded through clenched teeth, "You just forget you ever knew those people. They're nothing but trash. I don't want you to ever speak to them again".

No Longer a Victim

She pulled even harder on my hair, and said, "This disgraceful mess has got to go". She shoved me back in the seat and stared out the window.

She didn't say another word to me until the first stop we made. I saw a water fountain on the side of a building and went to take a drink. Above it was a sign that read, "Colored". I didn't have any idea what this meant. I started to take a drink when I felt myself being yanked away by my arm. I turned ready to punch whoever it was, but it was Mother. "What in the hell are you doing?" she asked. "I was getting a drink", wasn't that kinda obvious? "Not from the colored fountain you're not", she exclaimed with a haughty lift to her head. It was then I saw the other fountain with the sign above it that read, "Whites", and I realized my mistake. I drew myself up to my full height, which was only an inch or two shorter than Mother in her high heels, and looked her square in the eyes defiantly, daring her to try and stop me. I turned back and took a long drink from the fountain. Satisfied that I had made a statement that not only communicated my new found independence from my family's tyranny but also a stand in honor of Ferd and Chuck, I stood back up with a drawn out Ahhh... escaping my lips. I looked at Mother once again. She hesitated for a split second then fast as a whip her hand came toward my face. I had lightning fast reflexes as a result of my hours of training with Jonny and Roy, so I stopped her hand in mid-flight and held it tight. I spoke calmly, "Nobody's gonna hit me anymore, Mama". She stood for a few seconds with her mouth slightly open staring unbelievingly at my face. Then a momentary look of fearful uncertainty followed by acceptance softened her and she relaxed with a slight nod of her head.

No Longer a Victim

The rest of the trip was relatively peaceful. When we arrived at the bus station in Oklahoma City there was a man waiting to pick us up. I learned that he was my new step-father. His name was Randy. He was a big man with a broad chest and strong arms. He appeared a little older than Mother. His thick, dark hair was tinged with gray at the temples and his face was clean shaven. He looked me up-and-down as if deciding if I was going to cause him any trouble. I decided right then and there that I would.

It didn't take long for Mother to decide that her attempt at being a mom was in vain once again. She sent me back to live with Grandmother. Most of the family had moved out by this time. Aunt Mabel, Aunt Cheryl and Uncle Dave were all that was left. Grand Mother really wasn't happy about me being there, but she went along with it anyway. She appeared a bit taken off guard at first that the little boy who had disappeared more than 3 years before had returned looking like a young man with fire in his eyes. I guess she figured I would at least be another set of hands to help out with the work. I too was a little shocked when I first saw Grand Mother. She had aged considerably. Her shoulders were hunched over as if she was carrying a heavy burden all of the time. I guess, in a way, she was. Her long hair was all white and tied up in a tight bun at the back of her head. There were deep crevices around her mouth and eyes and the skin on her now thin face drooped as if it were being pulled down by some unseen force. Her eyes were as sharp as ever though and pierced me to the core. Her voice still commanded the fear of God and filled me with dread. I felt as if she had the power to sentence me to hell. My anger and hatred of God had started simmering at a young age as a result of my Grand Mother's condemning words. It had cooled some during my time in California, but facing the source of my animosity and resentment once again started the fire burning with a renewed intensity.

Dave was running the still now. He was glad to have a work animal to order around. I started drinking again right away because I saw no other way to escape what now seemed a hopeless future. Mabel decided she would try and mother me, but she gave up on that notion real quick when I responded with outright defiance. I think she was actually afraid of me. Of course the schools wanted nothing to do with me, so I stayed home most of the time.

I had taken to sleeping in the cellar. I don't know why exactly. Maybe it was because that had been the place Jonny found me and so it represented a shred of hope or at least a reminder that other, better places did exist. I'm not sure. Well, one night Uncle Ross came to check on

"Sprung From Hell"

the condition of the still. He and Dave got drunk. I could see that trouble was brewing. I remembered being five years old, alone, helpless and scared locked in the darkness shaking from fear and pain. I had promised myself that there would come a day when I would not allow anyone in my family to hurt me again. This time I would be prepared. The only thing I could find was a garden hoe, so it became my weapon of defense.

I had trouble falling to sleep. I jumped at every sound. Just when I had finally started to drift off I heard the cellar door being lifted. A strange calm came over me, a sort of excitement at the prospect of doling out some long deserved revenge. Dave tripped and cursed at the steps as if they were to blame for making him stumble. Ross shoved Dave out of his way and kicked at me to wake me up. I grabbed his foot and twisted it till he fell over. I jumped up while I had the chance. Dave started laughing till Ross got back on his feet and yelled at him to shut-up. Then he turned on me. "Who the hell do you think you are, you little shit? I'm gonna teach you a lesson you'll never forget". Dave still hadn't been able to maneuver himself to a standing position in his inebriated state, but he continued to try as he yelled obscenities of his own at me. Ross swung at my head and missed. This only angered him more. With his next swing he caught me in the gut. I doubled over as the breath was forced out of me. Ross grabbed me by the hair and pulled me upright. He unbuckled his belt and unzipped his pants with his free hand. I kicked him hard in the shin causing him to let loose of my hair. I scrambled to the place I had hidden my weapon. He was too drunk to realize that I was holding the hoe. His pants had dropped around his ankles by the time he crossed the small space between us. He reached to grab me with the intent of humiliating me again. I brought the head of the hoe up in an arc that caught and severed Ross' scrotum. He screamed so loud the sound resonated through Shanty Town. Blood went everywhere as he thrashed around in pain and shock. I stood transfixed with the hoe still in my grasp. Soon the cellar was surrounded by people who had been awakened by his screams. "Call the police and an ambulance", someone yelled.

Dave was wailing like he was the one who got hurt. Aunt Mabel got some old rags for Ross to try and stop the bleeding. Everyone was staring at me like I was an alien or something and a couple of men guarded the entrance to the cellar so I couldn't get out till the police came. Well, when they came they arrested me. Dave said I had attacked Ross. I thought, "How stupid can people be? Sure, I pulled his pants down so I could cut him. This was self defense! Why couldn't they see?" As

I was being taken away in hand cuffs, I saw Grand Mother standing off, away from the crowd of onlookers. She glared at me as if I was the devil himself. A cold shiver ran up my spine and turned my blood to ice. I actually felt relieved when they put me in the back of the police car and shut the door.

My trial was a joke, but not a funny one. Mabel had found a way to get back at me. She told the judge it was me who would lead Ross on. Aunt Cheryl, who never cared about anybody, told the judge I was gay. All Grand Mother did was stand in the court room and cry, "My son, my son". As for Mother, where, oh where could my mother be? I found out later she was pregnant with my baby brother. So, I guess she had better things to do.

I was sentenced to two years in juvenile detention. I still could not understand how I was sent to jail for defending myself.

♦ 11 ♦

Boys Ranch

I WAS SENT TO SEDAN, NEW Mexico, a little place out in the middle of nowhere. The guards loaded us on an old school bus that had been painted gray. The words "Department of Corrections" were painted on the side. We were herded onto the bus like cattle, our hands and feet chained. We were left without a shred of dignity as the guards pushed and shoved and yelled dehumanizing insults at us.

The ride was long and hot. We sat mostly in silence, sweating on the hard vinyl, seats, each lost in our own thoughts of despair and fear of the future that awaited us. The guards seemed to view us as sub-human, scum deserving of cruelty. Whenever we would stop to eat each of us got a dry cheese sandwich on stale white bread and a small carton of warm milk. The guards would order food from whatever diner we had stopped at. One time they sat right in front of us relishing juicy steaks and baked potatoes with all the trimmings. They would smack and sigh with satisfaction as loudly as they could and mock us as we choked down our less than appetizing and completely unsatisfying rations. I spoke up and suggested that they were nothing more than pigs. That only served to get my sandwich thrown on the ground and stomped on.

When we arrived we were introduced to the warden, Mr. Floyd Johnson. He was not a man to my liking. He lined us up on the side of the bus and informed us that he was to be our Mother, Father, sister and brother for the duration of our time at his ranch. He was right about one thing; he was a "mother". He barked out the list of rules and said there would be no mercy. Any infraction would be rewarded with an extension of our sentence. Needless to say, he and I didn't hit it off too well. Seemed he thought he was God and we were nothing but pagans. It was his job to pass on divine retribution.

Next we were given our cell assignments and marched into the cell block. That was when we met our Den Mother, the Cell Warden. Martin was his name. He walked down the line of prisoners with his hands clasped behind his back like he was some kind of big-shot. He stuck his big nose in each prisoner's face and stared him down. He didn't speak till he got to me. He looked at my name tag and then consulted the clipboard which he grabbed from his skinny, pale assistant.

"You got your hoe with you today?" he asked sarcastically. I looked him right in the eye and replied, "If I did, I know right where I'd shove it". Well, I spent my first night and 29 more in solitary confinement for that. I guess he thought I'd break down or something, but I actually preferred to be alone. Wake-up call at 4 am was not my cup of tea though. I was taken to the chow room with everyone else, but I sat alone and was not allowed to talk to anyone. Most of the other prisoners avoided eye contact with me, but occasionally I would get a glare or a curious glance.

The solitary cells were on the third floor. I could hear other prisoners being moved around periodically through the day. They would yell up to the guys in solitary. I never paid any attention to what they said or answered them back. I wasn't about to get myself involved in any situation with someone I couldn't see. There was a guy in the cell next to me named Henry. We weren't supposed to talk, which was fine with me, but this guy wouldn't shut-up. I found out that he lacked only two days till he was to return to the floor, which meant the main population. According to him that was like hell in a small place.

When my time in solitary was finished I was taken out to the yard. I remembered that Jonny and Roy always said, "If you have to fight, find the biggest guy you can and try to take him out. Win or lose you'll earn respect and most likely gain a friend". I stood off to the side for a while and watched closely how everyone interacted. There was a big, cowboy looking dude who seemed to be in charge. I heard another inmate address him as Buzz. By the size of him I knew my ass was as good as kicked, but there didn't to seem to be anyone else who fit.

Boys Ranch

I walked slowly up to him staring him in the eye. He maintained eye contact with me and I could see the wheels turning in his head. I was full of fear, but I willed my legs to keep going. I balled up my fist and swung at him like I was hitting a baseball. I landed a solid blow to his gut and he doubled over. With a knee lift I put him down. Well, that's about all I remember. All hell broke loose and I woke up in the hospital. My nose was broke and my ribs were cracked. There wasn't a spot on me that didn't hurt. I don't know how long I was in there, but as soon as I was able to walk I found myself facing the senior warden. He tacked 6 months on to my sentence and put me back in solitary for 30 more days. I figured that gave me time to recover before getting another beating, because I was certain that was what would happen as soon as I returned to the yard where Buzz was waiting.

"Sprung From Hell"

The day came all too soon. I walked cautiously down the hall and out the door into the glaring sun light. As my eyes adjusted I saw Buzz walking toward me. I flexed my fingers and stood tall and resolute. Maybe I would get beat again, but I would not back down from a fight. He stopped directly in front of me and just stared me down for several seconds without speaking a word. I was sure he was deciding what would be the fastest and most efficient way to kill me. Then he said, "The boys done a number on you. Are you okay?" I was dumbfounded. I didn't know what to say so I just nodded. He paused for a moment, and then asked, "Why did you hit me, I don't even know you?" I explained about what Jonny and Roy had taught me and said, "You seemed to be the best choice". A confused look passed momentarily across his face then a grin split his features and before long he was laughing hysterically. I joined in the hilarity and we emerged as best friends, just like Jonny and Roy had said would happen.

He pulled some strings and got me on barn detail with him. It turned out he had more influence than I had first thought. Because I was Buzz's friend the trouble stopped. Even the guards respected Buzz and so they were friendly to me.

For the first week I was the joke for everyone. I had worked at the milk factory when I was young, but I had never seen a bull. I asked, "Why don't this one come into the barn to get milked with the rest of the cows"? They all looked at me for a second, and then they burst out laughing. "Cause that's a bull", Buzz said between gasps, "I'd like to see you try to milk him".

One day the guards announced that they needed someone to run the fence line. I got volunteered. I had never ridden a horse before and I think the other guys knew it. When I got back that evening I felt like I had been beat with a paddle up and down my legs. "What's a matter boy?" one of the guys asked. "Why you walkin like you got a stick up your butt?" They really enjoyed that one.

As time went on I got to liking running the line. There was only one guard and two lowlies, me being one of them. It was hard work. We fixed the smaller holes and blocked off the larger ones. It felt so good to be out in the open. The sun and the breeze made me feel like I was free. I even enjoyed the work. My muscles were responding to the constant strain and becoming strong and flexible.

After we finished the smaller holes we went back to repair the ones we had blocked off. This time we took a truck. We loaded it down with fence poles and staples and stretchers and other such repair materials. Buzz was the driver. That year went by fast. Being a barny and a fencer was a satisfying life. I almost forgot that I was in jail.

Then the time came that Buzz's sentence was done. I dreaded the day that he left for good. We said goodbye with straight faces and hearty hugs complete with pounds on the back and slugs to the arms. Inside I was practically trembling with insecurity. Buzz had been my protector and friend. I wasn't sure what life would be like for me without Buzz around.

Turned out I had earned respect of my own with the other guys and even the guards. I was next in line to be the driver, but I was only 14 and had no license. Somehow they worked it out so I got a farm license. No more riding that dumb horse! Lawrence became the head lowlie in the barn and I got feed duty. I loaded up the hay and other feeds and ran them out to the stock. I liked this job because I did it alone. Although no body gave me any trouble and I was treated with respect I still had fears and insecurities down inside that would not go away. The recorded lines in my head were too deeply etched to erase. So, I kept up the pretense on the outside while I cowered in fear and isolation on the inside.

I was biding my time waiting to be done with my sentence and it seemed an eternity. Just when I was about to get a reduction in my time for good behavior a fight broke out in the mess hall. It didn't take long for the whole place to erupt in chaos. There were fists flying and guys falling all over the place. The floor was slimy with food spilled from overturned tables and blood from broken noses and busted lips. Now, you can't just sit in your seat and do nothing as all hell breaks loose around you so, I was right in the middle of it. That blew my shot at good behavior. I had to serve my full time. However, in the time that had passed the senior warden had actually started to like me a little. He gave me the job of taking Cookie, who was the cook, into town for supplies. This duty required a state license. So, at the age of 14 I had a real driver's license.

The truck I drove was a 1950 Chevy. It was in pretty sorry shape when I first got it, but it didn't take long till I had it running like a top. I enjoyed that old truck. It had been my companion for a long time and felt like an old friend. I hated to leave it behind, but the day came that I was released to return home.

Home; that was an interesting concept, in all the time I spent locked up, anticipating the day I would be free again, I hadn't considered where I would go. I thought about trying to find Jonny or Roy, but they didn't need the likes of me showing up fresh out of jail with nothing, asking them to take me in. I decided I had to go back to Oklahoma and try to make something of myself before going to California again.

The bus trip home was long and boring. We'd go 6 hours then stop, 2hours then stop, 4hours then stop. There was a 12 hour layover in Truth or Consequences, New Mexico. There is nothing to do or see in Truth or Consequences. I felt like I could have walked home faster.

I didn't eat much on the way either because they had only given me a few dollars upon my release. I was thankful for what I did have though. I thought briefly about stopping in Weaver, Texas to see if I had any relations there, but I decided pretty quickly that was just a fantasy.

When I finally got to Oklahoma I called home to see if anyone would care to come pick me up. Uncle Dave said he'd come. I waited for several hours, mulling over in my head whether I had made the right decision or not. I considered running a few times, but discarded that notion on account of having nowhere else to go. The future loomed uncertain once again and I waited.

♦ 12 ♦

Runnin' Red Eye

IT WAS A COUPLE HOURS BEFORE Dave showed up. He arrived in an old beat up pick–up that resembled the truck I had left at the boys' ranch. It helped, in some odd way, to settle my mind. I looked through the passenger window at Dave. Neither of us spoke a word. He nodded his head once as if to give nonverbal permission for me to get in the truck. I slid onto the seat and slammed the door sealing my fate. I had made my choice, now I would live with it.

Runnin' Red Eye

I noticed that I sat the same height as Dave in the truck seat. I actually took up more room than he did. I was only 15, but I was big, and a man to be reckoned with. I think Dave realized this fact too. He shifted around in the seat kind of like he was nervous. He reached over and fiddled with the radio for a while. I just watched him out of the corner of my eye. I was enjoying his discomfort. Finally, frustrated that he couldn't find any music to his liking, he shut off the radio and turned to me. "I never liked the way things went down", he admitted. "It wasn't right that you got sent up the river for defending yourself". I sat quietly for a few seconds, letting what he said sink in. I decided it was better to accept his offer of peace than to push the issue, so I nodded, indicating my ascent. We rode in silence for a time, and then he said, "You can run Red Eye with me if you want to".

"Sprung From Hell"

I nodded again and we finished the trip home without another word.

The family gave me a "49" Ford. The runs I made in the beginning were local and so didn't pay much. That was okay because I didn't need much. My life was different now. I was considered an adult and I was allowed access to places and activities that had formerly been forbidden. Suddenly I was getting attention from girls that wouldn't give me the time of day in school.

One weekend we had a party at the lake. I started off the evening with one girl, but as the hour got late and the booze was taking its toll I hooked up with another girl named June. Well June was Bobby's girl. When he found out he jumped me and started pounding my face. I wasn't about to take a beating, but I didn't want to hurt Bobby either. I understood his being mad, even though I didn't think she was worth it. I shoved him off me and planted a solid blow to his jaw. He fell to the ground with a thud. June ran up to me and started pounding her fists into my chest, and calling me a beast. I grabbed both her wrists and held her away from me. I told her she was nothing but a whore and I didn't know why Bobby wanted to be with her anyway. She ran off crying and none of us saw her again until morning when her body was found dangling from a tree. She had hung herself. We found out later she had been pregnant. Bobby blamed me, so we got into lots of fights after that.

The law was asking a lot of questions. They were hell bent on pinning her death on me. Of course I was feeling bad about what I had said to her. I knew my cruelty had something to do with her decision to take her life. Uncle Dave suggested that it would be good for me to get out of town for a while. There was a run that needed to be done to Gainesville, Tx. I jumped at the chance.

Dave told me to take my time, so stuff had a chance to settle down around home. I enjoyed the drive. The scenery was beautiful. I stopped in Turner Falls and saw my first bikinis, then went on to Gainesville. I made a pit stop at a bar and met a girl. She was the most beautiful creature I had ever seen. I knew I was in love. As the liquor loosened my tongue I bragged to her about the run I was making. I made sure she understood how dangerous it was and how brave I was to be taking the risk. I left to make the drop assuring her I would return, money in hand, to take her away with me.

Man, she was good, and man, was I stupid. I made the drop, got paid and got arrested one block away from the drop, by the very girl I had just fallen in love with. She kissed me on the cheek and said, "Thanks for the good time, baby". I felt the blood rising in my face. I had never felt so foolish. How could I have been so dumb? I vowed never to be duped by a pretty face again, as I was shoved into the back of the police car.

I knew, since I was still a minor that I wouldn't go to the big house, but Juvi hall was a very real possibility. I had heard stories at the ranch about Juvi. I wasn't too keen about going there. Just sitting in the holding cell was bad enough. I had seen some gangs in my day, but nothing like this. The Spanish hated the whites and the blacks. The blacks hated the whites and the Spanish. Hell, the whites hated everybody, and I didn't fit in anywhere. I stayed to myself and didn't make a sound. They left me alone except for an occasional glare.

After three days I was taken to court. Waiting for the judge seemed to take a lifetime, maybe because I could feel my life slipping into oblivion. Finally the judge came in. He sat down and read the report on his desk, glancing up at me occasionally. I began to feel more and more uncomfortable with each glance. He flipped through the papers one more time and then stared at me. I felt like I was a specimen under a microscope. "How old are you, son?" he asked. "Fifteen", I replied. He studied me for a few more seconds then said, "Well, I don't know how you managed to get a license nor do I care, but I have decided to let you go, seeing that this is the first offense of this kind you've been involved in and that you are from another state. There is, however one stipulation. You will never set foot in my jurisdiction again. Is that clear?" "Yes sir, your Honor, I promise". With that I was on my way home. I knew I had narrowly missed serving some real time in Juvi. I was free, boy, that felt good, a second chance.

Runnin' Red Eye

For the next couple of years I stuck to local runs and skirted the edge of trouble. I partied a lot. Everyone invited me to their parties because they knew I would bring the booze.

I had gotten my GED while I was in the Boys Ranch, so I was free from having to go to school. I spent my free time working on bikes. I never lost my love for them. People from all over would bring their bikes to me. I developed a reputation as the guy who could fix anything on two wheels, bicycles to motorcycles. I was content with making small runs every now and then, but my uncles were constantly after me to go back to Texas. They wanted me to go because they didn't want to take the risk themselves. I continued to refuse until Uncle Dave pointed out that one run to Gainesville would pay for the car of my dreams. It was a 1957, Ford Fairlane with a convertible hard top.

"Sprung From Hell"

Man, I wanted that car. I thought about it for a good while before I agreed.

I knew I was taking a huge chance, but I was older and wiser this time. I wouldn't make the same mistake again. I did stop to look at the bikinis at Turner Falls again, but got back to business right after that.

Once I was in Gainesville I took two days to scope out the drop. I was being extra careful this time. I didn't see any indication that there was a set-up this time. I waited till after dark anyway and pulled up across the street a few houses down. I cut the engine and watched the house.

Everything was quiet, maybe a little too quiet. A misty rain had begun to fall giving an eerie feel to the scene. A stray cat bolted out from under a parked car and caused me to jump. I shook my head and said to myself, "This is ridiculous, I'm scared by a cat? It's now or never".

Runnin' Red Eye

I got out of the truck and pulled my collar up to keep the mist off my neck. I walked across the street and climbed the steps to the house. I knocked on the door. Next thing I knew I was being shoved up against the wall and frisked as an officer read my rights and hand-cuffed me. To this day I don't know what went wrong. I was taken to jail again and all I could think was, "I hope I don't get the same judge". I was in holding again for four days. They finally came to take me to court. My face drained of all color as I watched the same judge enter and take his seat at the bench. I knew I was going down for sure this time.

The judge looked at me for a long time then asked, "Do I know you"? I answered with a tentative, "I don't think so". He just eyed me suspiciously. He said, "I could send you to Huntsville for twenty years, you know?" What I feared most was about to happen to me.

"Sprung From Hell"

My head was swimming and I thought I might pass out like a girl right there in the court room. However, in the 1950's the draft was still in effect. So, the United States military became my saving grace. "I'll give you the choice, either you sign up for the service or I'll send you away for a very long time", he offered. I agreed immediately and they signed me up right then and there.

I chose the Army infantry. I was already a pretty good shot with a gun and so that seemed the way to go. On the way home I was thinking that I would be the only member of the family who had ever served in the military, besides Uncle Ray, but I didn't know much about him. I was actually excited about this new venture. Perhaps it would be a good thing after all.

♦ 13 ♦

Soldier Boy

THE FIFTH OF JULY WAS THE BIG day. Mother actually appeared to be proud of me. She fussed over my hair being cut straight and combed just so. She brushed imaginary lint off my clothes and sighed a lot. At moments I would catch her with a small tear in the corner of her eye. I didn't quite know how to handle this new side of my mother. Part of me wanted to believe it was genuine, but the walls around my emotions had been refortified too many times for a little tear to make any difference.

"Sprung From Hell"

Even Grandmother was acting like she cared. She called Uncle Ray to come down for a visit and tell me just what I was in for. He lectured me on discipline and respect as he marched back and forth in front of me like he was the commander and chief. I listened, but all the while I was thinking that I learned more about respect and discipline and what it means to be a man from Roy and Jonny than he could even dream of knowing.

The big day dawned bright and clear. Well, actually I had already been up for several hours before the dawn, but when it came it was bright and clear. I felt as if the light and warmth were seeping right into my chest. I was happier than I could ever remember being. We drove in silence to where the buses were waiting.

There must have been 100 guys there ready to pledge their lives to protecting our great nation, or perhaps they were just escaping jail time like me. It didn't matter; we were heading out on the biggest adventure of our young lives. Some were wearing white undershirts with no sleeves standing off apart from the others blowing smoke from their hand-rolled cigarettes like the stacks on top of big factories. They were trying to look indifferent. I guess to prove they weren't afraid of anything the military could dish out. Others wore starched, white, collared shirts with their ties drawn up under their chins. They were mostly accompanied by who I assume were their parents. Men in business suits and women in fancy dresses and heels who acted like they were afraid some commoner might touch them and soil their reputation. Still others wore plaid, button up shirts and trousers that were too short. Many of them looked as if they might cry any minute and run home to mommy.

Then there was me. I wore old jeans with a tear in the knee and a faded t-shirt.

"Sprung From Hell"

I was taller than everyone there and though bursting with excitement on the inside I stayed cool on the outside. I eyed each group in turn communicating with a look that I wanted to be left alone.

Time came to load the buses. I said a hasty goodbye to my Mother, who put on a good show of sniffling and waving a handkerchief, settled into the hard seat and dreamed of the glory that awaited me.

Ft. Dix became a place I was not very fond of. They treated us like blue-tick dogs that wouldn't hunt. We were apparently all lazy, no good, momma's boys who couldn't even wipe our own asses. Anyway, I did get something I had never had before, two pairs of new boots and a pair of dress shoes and lots of new clothes that were not hand-me-downs. I learned how to spit shine those boots till you could see your reflection from a mile away and make a bed that could bounce a quarter from here to Mexico. I suppose the regimented life gave me a sense of security. I knew exactly what was expected of me and I could excel at most of it. Nothing was left to chance everything was planned. I had only to follow orders. That way there was no chance for the half-wit, which still lurked in my subconscious, to botch something up.

I was transferred to Ft. Bliss for Basic Training and then to Ft. Hood for A/T training. I grew physically as-well-as intellectually. I learned about weapons I never knew existed and how to use them. I learned a lot about our great nation and the principles it was founded on. For the whole time at basic we had the Core Values drilled into our heads. There are 7 of them and they form the acronym LDRSHIP; Loyalty, Duty, Respect, Selfless Service, Honor, Integrity and Personal Courage. I was accustomed to most of them because the life of a biker is very similar to the military. I thrived

"Sprung From Hell"

on the physical exertion and marveled at the changes in my body.

The majority of our time was spent marching and standing in formation and practicing drill ceremonies. The road marches were not my cup of tea, but I did them anyway. One thing I couldn't get used to was the yelling in my face. So, I also learned how to scrub a bathroom with a toothbrush.

Once I busted a Corporal in the mouth with a pretty good blow. The whole platoon got extra duty for that. The other guys didn't take too kindly to being punished for my temper, so they got even. I was invited to a "Blanket Party". In the wee hours of the morning, contentedly sawing logs in my bunk, when all of the sudden my blanket was wrapped around my whole body and I was hoisted out of bed. I was disoriented and groggy and couldn't see a thing. I could feel each blow through the thin blanket though.

Fists, boots and various blunt objects were repeatedly thrust into my body. I couldn't fight back and I felt the familiar suffocating fear of being trapped. Then, it stopped, as suddenly as it had begun. The fear melted away and was replaced by rage. I thrashed around until I was free of the blanket. Cold air hit me in the face with a jolt. I realized I was alone and outside in nothing but my underwear. I looked around frantically, but there was no one around. I started to shiver as the cool night air blew on my sweaty body. I was struck with the thought of how silly I must look. I deserved what I got and it really was pretty funny. I was sore, but I had certainly received worse beatings in the past. I started to chuckle and then broke out in all out laughter. Mysteriously guys started to emerge from the shadows laughing right along with me. We exchanged some good natured slugs and slaps on the back. "You really can take a beating like a man", one guy said. "You're alright, man. I hope if I ever see combat I've got guys like you watching my back", another said. Many others grunted their agreement. A bond was formed between us that night. Brotherhood is a marvelous thing and it felt great.

One thing I excelled at was weaponry. I was an expert with pistols and rifles. I earned the title of sharp-shooter with an M-1 rifle. Being their prize shooter got me out of some serious trouble once. Our drill sergeant's name was Sgt. Cafry. Now, Sgt. Cafry had no love for me and he wasn't my favorite person either, but I was the best shooter on his team, so he put-up with me. One morning we were running a drill called leap-frog boundary. We would line up in rows of two. The idea was for every other guy to leap over his partner's back and shoot then immediately duck so his partner could leap his back and shoot and so-on. This particular day Sgt. Cafry and I were partners and I had been issued an old M-1 rifle. It got jammed. Instead of "leaping", like I was supposed to, I stayed put and tried to un-jam my gun. Sgt. Cafry turned to see why I had not jumped just as I got the gun un-jammed and a shot fired missing his head by inches.

We stared at each other for a few bewildered seconds before he let loose a stream of cuss-words that would have embarrassed a sailor and came at me with fists flying. I easily dodged his punch and one of the other guys grabbed him and held him back. He looked like he had just woken up from a bad dream with wild eyes and flailing arms. Some of the other guys and me were laughing which only served to piss him off more. Finally I said, "Let him go". He lunged forward and landed a sloppy punch to my jaw. I just looked at him and asked, "Are you done now"? Out of breath and dizzy from the ringing in his ear he replied with a weary, "Yes", and slumped to the ground. I lifted him to his feet and said, "I wasn't trying to kill you, if I'd a been tryin, you'd be dead". Then I warned him, "I let you hit me cause I deserved it, but don't ever try it again". I helped him walk to the jeep so they could take him to the infirmary. He never said a word and there was never any disciplinary action taken. I can only assume that it was due to my shooting record that I wasn't punished severely.

It wasn't long till we got our orders. I was going to Augsburg, Germany. The thought of leaving the U.S. filled me with dread. Old feelings of uncertainty and self-doubt surfaced again. A new country a new culture, what if I couldn't fit in, what if there were new standards I couldn't live up to? What made me think I had any chance of succeeding? Then a new thought struck me. What if I didn't like German women, or what if they didn't like me? Now, I had known my share of women. There were always girls hanging around the bars near military bases. They all had their minds set on being officer's wives. They were more than willing to give out samples of the goods. I had a view of women that was a mixture of awe and contempt. I saw them as objects to be used for pleasure, but to be kept at a distance because they had strange powers that could capture a man's soul. I had seen it happen to more than one guy. The thought of a future without them though would be quite bleak, so I got drunk.

My mother came to bid me farewell. That turned into a disgusting nightmare. In a state of inebriation I whined to her about missing American women. You remember that my mother used sex to make things okay. That had always been her answer. So, she offered herself to me. When she got that look in her eye and started approaching me, while unbuttoning her blouse, something exploded in my heart. It was a pain like none I had felt before, like a blackness was growing in my chest and would consume my entire being. The filth, the shame, the fear all came rushing in. What in the hell was wrong with me? I felt myself shrinking from the knowledge of my own grotesque state and I had to get away. I screamed, "No!", and ran from the room leaving her standing with her shirt open and her own shame staring her in the face. I went straight to a bar and got into a fight with the first person I heard use the term, "Mother-f*****".

My time in Germany turned out to be one of the best times in my life. The first six months were hard work. I had to prove myself to the new company. Most of the guys had been there for a while and already knew each other. I was the new kid so everyone wanted a piece of me. Even the little guys pushed me around to see what I was made of. I stayed cool most of the time because the military was all I had and I was determined not to screw it up.

The colonel read my records and saw that I was good with a rifle. He put me to the test on the range and was very impressed. I became his special weapon. We went to competitions with German army units and I usually won. That got me promoted, but then my drinking and fighting would get me demoted. It turned out German women were pretty much the same as American women except you didn't have to worry about them wanting you to "talk" and "share your feelings" because they couldn't speak English and I couldn't speak German. That suited me just fine.

The two years went by fast and it was time to ship home. The company Commander said he didn't want me to

"Sprung From Hell"

go home with the same rank I had come with. He told me to go to the PX and buy a stripe for a Private First Class, but not to sew it on till the day before my discharge. I went to the PX and saw all the stripes and emblems and decided to promote myself a little higher than the commander intended. I got stripes for a Master Sergeant, a Major Leaf, and stripes for 23 years of service and 21 years combat. When I stepped off the plane my mother asked, "What are you supposed to be?" I stood at attention and saluted as I stated that I was a Command Sergeant Major. She said, "You're a command clown, now get out of that uniform and quit embarrassing me". I had put our last meeting out of my head and the little boy inside me honestly thought she would be proud of me, but I guess I pushed it a bit too far.

◆ 14 ◆

Settling Down

I WAS BACK TO MY FORMER WAY of life and it did not seem promising. I started back in drinking hard and heavy. I did join the reserves. It took up two weekends per month. One weekend was combat training, the other just more drills and marches. It didn't pay me enough to cover the bills, so I tried to find a job. I tried everything; carpentry, plumbing, a lumber yard, even tried working on bikes, but my drinking caught up with me sooner or later no matter what I was doing. Life had no purpose and there was no hope for anything better. It was easier to be in a stupor all the time than it was to be sober and face the futility of my existence. I eventually went back to running moonshine. That was what I knew and it provided an endless supply of liquor. Trouble was I drank more than I sold and I still couldn't pay the bills.

During this time I ran into Alice. She had been around Shanty Town for years. We had attended school together. But, she wasn't a little girl anymore. She had grown up nicely. She was taller than most women, about 5'7" I guess, but still 8 or so inches shorter than me. She was slender, but curvy with shoulder length, wavy, blonde hair that she pinned back so it curled around her ears, and her pretty green eyes were framed by sweeping long lashes. She never wore makeup, she didn't need it anyway, and she always wore soft, light colored dresses with flowing skirts that went to below her knees. The thing that really got me though was the way she carried herself. It was a quiet confidence I saw in her. She didn't need any of the adornment other women used to get men's attention. I was a little surprised she would even talk to me. I treated her differently than I had ever treated a woman. She was pure, like new fallen snow or a fragile flower bud. This was the one time I had a chance to have something truly good in my life and I didn't want to screw it up.

I decided that running Red Eye was not the best choice if I wanted Alice to stay with me, so I went to work with my step-father installing insulation. I hated the work. It was hot and itchy and we were always two or three hundred feet in the air on scaffolds. One day my step-brother, Vernon, was working above us. All of the sudden we hear a scream like someone is dying. Vernon had tripped and was falling. I watched as my 5'7" step-dad reached out and caught his son by the work-belt and pulled him to safety on our scaffold. None of us spoke for several minutes. We were in a state of shock and disbelief that he had actually caught him in mid-air. I decided that day maybe I needed to look for another form of employment.

Once the shock wore off we were back to work as usual. Mother was always on my case to get married and settle down. I was too crazy and what I needed was a good woman to calm me down. My step-dad agreed. "You're gonna wind up in the pen if you don't make a change, boy", he warned.

I was terrified to ask Alice. Why would someone like her ever want to be with the likes of me, but I knew I had to make a move soon or I might lose her for good. I borrowed some money from my step-father and bought a ring with a small diamond on it at a pawn shop. I

Settling Down

felt like an ugly, dirty, stray dog going up to beg for a scrap from a pretty girl. I was exposing my heart at the risk of it being trampled. I couldn't even look at her in the eye. I got down on one knee on her parent's front porch and held out the ring. She said, "Did you have something you wanted to ask me?" I swallowed the lump in my throat and barely whispered, "Would you be my wife?" It took a couple of seconds for me to realize that she had said, "Yes", because I was bracing myself for the rejection that was sure to come. I looked up slowly and saw her smiling. I couldn't believe it. I picked her up and twirled her around yelling at the top of my voice, "She said, Yes". She slapped at my arm and sternly said, "Put me down". I wish I had realized that this was a sign of things to come, but I was too dizzy with the prospect of having a bright future to care.

We had a small ceremony in the Baptist church where she attended faithfully. Her parents and siblings were there as were my mother, step-father and step-brother. It was very solemn and too long for my taste, but my mind was on the wedding night, not what the preacher was saying. My mother baked a small cake and we drank some kind of punch out of paper cups then we were off to our "honeymoon", which was actually just a one bedroom apartment I rented, over the garage of my folk's place.

While she was in the bathroom I stole a few swigs of red-eye from the bottle I had stashed. I was actually nervous. She came out wearing a long, white nightgown with a matching robe tied at the waist and buttoned up to her throat. I thought she looked like an angel. I walked to her and took her in my arms. "You look beautiful, baby", I whispered. As I leaned down to kiss her I reached

Settling Down

for the sash on her robe to untie it. She slapped my hands and drew back as if I had struck her. "What on earth are you doing?" she asked. I was totally caught off guard. "I was gonna take your robe off", I stammered. "You most certainly will not", she commanded. "What did you think, that I was going to be your own personal play thing?" "Well, I am not! We will not have sexual relations until we are prepared to have children. And that will not be until God says so." I could not believe my ears. Did she just say what I think she said? Confused, I asked, "Just how will you know when that happens?" The Bible will tell me", she stated matter-of-factly, as if any idiot should know that. She then asked me to turn around while she removed her robe and got into bed. I was dumbfounded. I snatched my bottle from its hiding place and went outside to get drunk.

"Sprung From Hell"

The next day at work my step-father wouldn't leave me alone. He kept asking how it was and if she was good in bed. Finally, when I couldn't take it anymore, I told him we had not done it yet. He stood there with his mouth open for a few seconds before he asked, "Why not?" I made up an excuse, "She was exhausted and didn't feel well." "Oh, okay", was all he said. The next day he asked me again. I told the same story. The next day was the same. By the fifth day my blood was boiling. I had been drinking a lot and I was tired of the looks I was getting from him and Vernon, who was in on the joke as well. "Bet you got a lot of "pressure" in your life about now, huh Kenner?" He laughed so hard he almost fell again. He was lucky I couldn't reach him because I would have pushed him.

I stormed away from the work site and got in my truck. What in the hell was happening to me. I practically had

Settling Down

women throwing themselves at me in Germany. Why was I letting Alice make an ass out of me? I was a joke to my step-father because of her. She was my wife, I was the man. No woman was going to run my life. She would do as I said or else! I pulled the bottle out from under the seat and took a long drink. "By damned, that woman will obey me!" I screeched away from the curb determined to lay down the law. By the time I got home I had finished the bottle and my brain was a bit foggy. Doubts were nagging me. "What if she's right? What if God really did talk to her? She was the only thing I had ever had that wasn't tainted in some way. Then I saw an image in my mind of my step-father and Vernon laughing at me. A split second thought crossed my mind, what would Jonny and Roy and the other guys think of me now?" My rage was rekindled. No way was a woman going to run my life.

"Sprung From Hell"

I slammed the truck door and headed straight up the stairs. When I stomped into the room she gasped in surprise. Her eyes widened as she asked cautiously if everything was alright. "No, it isn't", I yelled. "You're my wife and I will have you. "She backed away from me, the fear showing on her face. "No, Kenner, it's not right. "It's right if I say it's right", I shouted. I shoved her onto the bed and ripped open her dress. She started to whimper and tears trickled down her face. I felt myself softening and this only enraged me more. I slapped her across the face and told her to shut-up. I had my way with her and she did not protest any further. I left her curled up in a fetal position on the bed sobbing quietly, and went to buy another bottle.

I stayed drunk for two days and slept in my truck. I didn't even show my face at the job site. Guilt over what I had done was eating me up inside. The voices in

Settling Down

my head would not shut up, no matter how much I drank. "You're a no good half-wit for sure. The family was right all along. You screw up everything you touch." They would not stop. I had to get away, I couldn't stay there anymore, that was for sure.

The only thing I had been successful at was the military, so I went to see the recruiter. He asked me what my goals were. I told him I wanted to be an officer. He looked over my records and said if I could up my score on the G.E.D. I could do just about anything I wanted. So, I started studying. I wasn't going to hang around home though. I decided to go to California and look up Jonny and Roy.

They were easy to find. Jonny was the president of the club. I went to the old clubhouse and there they were. They were glad to see me and gave me a place to stay while I studied. I found time to hang out and party too. I got reacquainted with guys I hadn't seen in years and made some new friends too. It was like old times, except Delia wasn't there. I found out that she had died of an overdose shortly after I left. I admit, I cried. She had been the only real Mom I had. I attacked my studies with fervor. I intended to do well in honor of her.

I passed the G.E.D. with flying colors. In fact I was in the top five of my class. From there it was off to basic training again, this time at Ft. Polk. I didn't like it any more than I did the first time, but at least I knew what to expect. They sent me to Ft. Brigg for flight training. I loved flying, but I could never get used to jumping out of the planes. It seemed ridiculous to me to jump when the plane was running just fine. My jumping instructor didn't like me at all, but that was okay because I didn't like him either. He pushed me the first time I jumped. I was so scared I almost forgot to pull the

Settling Down

rip cord. I survived though and successfully jumped four more times to earn my wings. Then I was off to Maryland for Officer Candidate School. I worked hard and graduated second from the top. Next was Ft. Sill and then back to Ft. Brigg for more flight training. I didn't jump out of any perfectly good planes this time, I actually flew them. Then at Ft. Benning I learned to fly a Huey cargo helicopter. That was cool! They taught us about flight missions and air assault styles. It was not easy for me. I had to study hard, not like some guys who seem to just breeze through and never crack a book. I fought for every bit of knowledge I acquired. It paid off, I was 25 yrs. old and going to Nam as an officer.

I now had a son as a result of me raping my wife. He was almost 4 and I had seen him only once. The military sent me home for 2 weeks when he was born. We had named him Kenneth Scott.

He looked just like me. It scared me to death when I looked at his little face and saw myself looking back at me. I went back thinking, "Boy, I have really messed up my life". I never really wanted to have kids in the first place.

Well, now I was going home for thirty days to spend time with my family before going to Nam. Alice had gained a lot of weight since the last time I saw her. She was no longer the pretty young girl I had been so taken with. She was tired and lonely and bitter. I guess I couldn't blame her. I was the cause of her miserable life. She was living with my mother and working as a helper to a salad chef at O.U. I slept on the couch for a few days and tried to connect with my son. I found that I was not gifted at relating to a toddler, so I left and started sleeping in my truck. For a week I listened to my Mother and Step-father constantly telling me I was a failure as a father. It

Settling Down

was my responsibility to make this marriage work for my son. I bought a bottle to give me some courage and went to try and work it out with Alice.

She was in no mood to hear me talk about how we needed to fix our relationship for our son. She had too much resentment pent up inside her to even listen to me. She spewed out toxic words that cut me to the core of my being. I knew she was right, that she was justified in her anger and hatred for me, but her words were slashing into my soul and conjuring up emotions from my past that had been buried for some time. The familiar rage started to boil up and coupled with the liquor I had drunk earlier it spilled over. I raped her again in an attempt to show that I was still a man and could control my wife, when in reality I was out of control. I left that night for Oakland.

♦ 15 ♦

Colors and Nam

I WAS DETERMINED TO START A new life. Everything I owned was in a leather knap-sack in my truck and I hit the open road on the way to the only place I had ever felt at home. I hooked up with Roy and his new old lady. She wasn't Delia, but she was cool. I met Doc and his family and we hit it off right away. Of course Mums and I struck up our friendship as if I had never left. Roy and some of the others wanted to sponsor me for membership, but there wasn't time for the usual prospecting, which took at least three months, so I had to go through an initiation process.

We were hanging out at the club house playing pool. I was drinking whiskey and playing rather well. I had a cute hang-around wearing nothing but a pair of cut off jeans and a leather vest holding my drink while I played. Man! Life was good!

Next thing I know, Mums is calling for a punching contest. He turned around and elbowed me right in the nose. Blood spurted out all over my face. I was instantly shocked and ticked-off at the same time. He stood there looking at me with a stupid grin. I broke the pool cue I was holding and swung at his head with the butt end of it. He ducked and I hit Animal by mistake. Well, he came after me, but I grabbed his shoulders and head-butted him. Then Billy grabbed a hold of me and I became a punching bag. One after the other, blow after blow, each one making me more angry than the last. With fury and searing pain shooting through my body I fought back till Billy let go. I knew I was about to explode. I could feel the pressure building in every cell of my body. I had to get out. These were my only friends and the men I wanted to call brothers. I needed to be a part of their world. I started for the door without saying a word. Madman stepped in front of me. "Where are you going", he demanded. Now, this was a mountain of a man. He was 6'7" and 360 lbs of pure muscle. I knew better than to hit him, so I said, "I can't fight you. I'm just tired of the fun". He looked down at me and simply said, "Turn around". I turned slowly, not sure what to expect and there stood Jonny, holding my colors. "You're now an honorary member of the club", he announced. I couldn't believe my eyes. He walked over and put the vest on me and pounded me on the shoulder. "You deserve it, brother", he said with just a touch of emotion in his

Colors and Nam

voice. He looked me in the eye for a split second and communicated the bond we had, then suddenly he was the president again. He turned and walked away confidently waving his arm in the air as he commanded, "Rack em up".

Not even the army gave me that kind of rush. I finally felt like I was really a part of something that mattered. Mums sauntered up to me and said, "That aint all". He motioned for me to follow him outside. In the front lot stood Madman, with a scooter that looked like something out of a Frankenstein movie. "You can't be a biker without a bike", he announced. They had pieced together parts from several bikes and scooters and made me a bike. I couldn't tell you what color it was, because it was several different colors. I can't even tell you what was holding it together. It looked like it might come apart if you hit a pot hole. The seat had holes in it, the grips didn't match, the tires were worn, but it was the most beautiful ride I had ever seen. It wasn't a Harley (well maybe parts of it were) but it was mine and I loved it. I let out a Yahoo! At the top of my voice and said, "Let's ride". Several of the guys mounted up and we took off for a couple of hours just cruising and feeling free. For the next few days I was on a high that nothing could bring me down from.

After that I didn't see Jonny much since he was the president and I was just a rooky. He spoke to me a couple of times, but for the most part Mums and Wild Bill were tasked with keeping an eye on me. Mums and Bill had both earned what was called the "Hardcore" patch, which basically meant you didn't want to mess with them. Jonny figured they would keep me from getting hurt seeing as how I was a "Hero" and all. Well, I wasn't one yet, but I was determined to be. I would make the brothers proud that they had accepted me into their ranks.

I spent the next two weeks enjoying my new status and learning to ride Mums' way, fast and hard. I stayed with Doc and his old lady, Hannah. We formed a tight bond over that short time. They took me to Oakland Army Base on a Sunday and I was bound for Vietnam the next day. I was young, strong, a full patch and scared out of my wits. What on earth made me think I could ever be a hero?

We touched down on a dirt airstrip in the middle of the jungle in a place called Buen-Hue. As I exited the plane the heat and humidity hit me in the face like a blast from a furnace. My starched uniform was instantly limp and sweaty. We marched about a half mile to the camp, which consisted of army green tents arranged in rows around the dirt yard used for assemblies. It was surrounded on every side by dense, green jungle.

The silence was eerie, even though there were actually sounds all around me. I felt like there was a presence lurking in the jungle watching us and it sent a shiver up my spine.

We stood at attention in the yard to be inspected and instructed by our company commander. He was a big man with a booming voice. He was around 45yrs. old and marched along the rows of soldiers with an authoritative confidence that gave us some measure of assurance. We were assigned to our tents and instructed to eat and get some rest because the wake-up call came at 4:00 AM and then our briefing started at 5:00.

Since I was now an officer, 2nd Lieutenant, I got assigned to the officer's quarters. All that meant was my tent was slightly larger and I didn't have to share with anyone. That was just fine with me. Inside the green tent there was a green cot with a green blanket and pillow, a green, canvas folding chair, a green, canvas stool that served as a side table and a green army trunk. It was very green. I deposited my gear in the trunk and went to find out what was on the menu at the mess tent.

The mess tent was just that, a larger version of our sleeping tents with sides that could be rolled up to let a breeze blow through, if there ever was a breeze, which was never. There were several rows of rectangular, metal tables with benches attached to their sides that could be folded up quickly and thrown in a truck for evacuation. They looked like they had been on the front lines rather than sitting in a tent. There was the hum of conversation in the air with the occasional loud laughter as the guys tried to enjoy their meals and each other's company ignoring the fact that they were thousands of miles from home in the middle of a jungle.

"Sprung From Hell"

I sat down at the officer's table to enjoy my slop on a piece of toast and my coffee that tasted like it had been brewed in an old boot. The Commander asked me if I was ready to fly. "Yes Sir, sure am", I replied. "Good! Get some sleep; I'll see you in the morning soldier." He stood up and clapped me on the shoulder with an almost sad look on his face, like he knew something I didn't know. I went to bed that night exhausted, but my dreams were disturbed by images of his face and a foreboding feeling that there was something terrible coming my way.

At 4:00 Am there was a loud siren blasted over the loud-speaker followed by a crackling voice announcing that formation was in 30 minutes. The siren jolted me out of my restless dreams and I rolled out of my cot landing with a dusty thud on the dirt floor. I cursed and struggled to untangle myself from the blanket. Minutes later I had brushed the dirt from my body washed my face and shaved and emerged from my tent ready to start my first day. Breakfast consisted of some kind of mush they tried to call oatmeal and more bad coffee. We had to eat it so fast we couldn't really taste it anyway, so it didn't matter.

At 5:00 we were all lined up in the yard to be inspected and to receive our assigned duties. We dispersed and went to the various places we were told to go. I sat in the briefing tent with several other guys. Each of the others was assigned to a flight pilot for instruction. I sat and I waited, but my name was not called. When the Commander asked if there were any questions I inquired as to where my flight pilot might be. He said, "Oh, we are going to "wing-span" you today", which I found out, basically means, on-the-job training. "I'll talk you into flight and my Tail Commander will talk you into a dive and how to pull out."

"I'll show you some of the countryside on the way back". Sounded easy enough, till we got to the heli-pad. They had Cobras, I had never seen a Cobra much less flown one. I was trained to fly a Huey.

The Commander didn't seem to think this was a big deal. He showed me how to lift, lower, swing and hover and from there we were on our way. We flew about 50 minutes and then the Commander's voice came over the radio, "Okay, now watch me and do the same as I do". He lowered and swung left, shooting all the way. Our target was in plain sight, so it was easy to spot. The two choppers in front of me did the same thing. It felt like I was watching a movie, but in 3-D with surround sound. This was no movie though, it was real, and I was pumped up on adrenaline as I prepared to dive. The command came over the radio, "Okay, now it's your turn". I lowered and swung left firing both rockets.

Colors and Nam

Everything seemed to be going fine till I saw a flash and felt a wave of heat like hell itself had exploded behind me. I was falling fast, like a ball of flame flashing through the sky. I tried with all my might to hold to the friendly side, but the force of the falling giant was too much to control. In panic I launched my seat not knowing where I would land. There was another explosion and I felt fire piercing through my body. I landed hard and felt a dizzying wave of nausea as I struggled to release my seat.

I heard voices in the tall grass nearby, but couldn't understand a word they were saying. Next thing I knew I was surrounded by Vietnamese soldiers pointing guns at my head. One of them poked me with his gun and shouted at me. I couldn't understand his words, but I understood his meaning. I was their prisoner. I stood to my feet with my mind racing frantically to find a way out. I had so much adrenaline pumping through my veins I didn't even notice my injuries. I lunged at the closest guy and laid him out with one punch. I turned to face the next opponent, but before I could reach him I was struck with a rifle across my lower back. I dropped to my knees and was kicked in the stomach with a muddy boot. I fell face first into the grass. They tied my hands behind my back and jerked me to my feet.

I was prodded like a cow in a slaughter shoot to a place in the jungle where several other men were tied up being guarded by more Vietnamese soldiers. Immediately we were lined up and forced to march. With each step my injuries became more painful. I had been showered with shrapnel when my chopper exploded in mid-air. The blood had begun to congeal, but each time I fell or stumbled I was kicked or beat with a gun reopening the wounds. The other guys were no better off than me. After hours of marching in the heat without water we finally stopped for a rest. I learned from the man next to me that he had been captured the day before when he got separated from his unit. He didn't know about the others. That was the last conversation we had because the Vietnamese soldier closest to us banged him in the back of the head with the butt of his gun for talking and knocked him out.

One of the guys signed to our captors that he was thirsty and the soldier answered in broken English, "Oh, you want drink, huh?" He laughed as he unzipped his pants and urinated on the man. The others saw this and decided to join in the fun. We all got showered with urine as they shared a good laugh. One of the soldiers lowered his pants and defecated right next to me. I shoved him with my shoulder causing him to fall over. This infuriated him. He kicked me repeatedly and then smeared his feces in my face. The stench made me gag and I wretched on the ground in front of me.

We were treated worse than animals. They marched us through the dense foliage for hours at a time. They gave us only enough water to keep us alive. We were locked in small metal cages at night and some were forced to carry them during the day. Occasionally they would separate one of us from the rest of the group and try to get information out of us. Only a couple of them spoke any English at all and that was very broken. I could not understand what they were asking for, but I wasn't about to give them any information anyway. I'm not sure if anyone else broke down. I honestly could not blame them if they did. We had our finger nails pulled out with pliers and were cut with dull knives. The beatings happened repeatedly every day. If they knew you had a wound that was

Colors and Nam

beginning to close they would gouge it to make it bleed again. We lost two men on the way. They were left in the rice patties to rot.

After three days infection had set into my wounds. Every step was a struggle. I had fever and would break out in cold sweats even though the temperature was over 100. My body was racked with pain and every fiber of my being cried out in agony. At first I had been filled with rage and looked for any opportunity to escape, but as dehydration and exhaustion and pain took their toll, hopelessness set in.

By the fourth day I had begun to lose touch with reality. Delirium was my constant companion. The faces of my torturers became faces from my past. I heard the voices of my family and others who had hurt me as a child distorted into demonic groaning and hisses. They lashed me with their tongues and cut me with their eyes. The fires of hell were licking at my feet. The horrific sounds of tortured souls screaming, the roar of flames, the loud crashing of rocks tumbling into the lake of fire. This was the end!

A voice, unlike the others, "Hey man, are you okay?" "No", I replied. The next thing I remember is waking up in a hospital bed with a Major looking intently at my face. "I'm glad to see you", he said, "You are lucky to be alive". I learned over the next few days that The Marines had ambushed the Vietnamese who had captured us. The sounds I heard must have actually been the sounds of battle. I and the others had been air-lifted to Tokyo. They had removed 126 pieces of shrapnel from my body. I was being treated for severe infection and dehydration, but the doctor said I should be fine. They said I was a POW for four days, it felt like an eternity.

There was a guy in the bed next to me in the hospital. I asked him what he was there for. He showed me his hand all bandaged up. He said he had cut it opening a can of beans with a P-38. I thought that was crazy. A few days later we found out that Gen. Leland was coming to give out medals. The man who actually came to hand out the medals was a captain named Happy. He started reading off the list of medals. Some got the Silver Star along with a Purple Heart. He announced that the Major who had cut his hand on a can of beans was getting a Purple Heart. I got a Bronze Star and a Meritorious Service Award and A Purple Heart. I told him where he could put his Purple Heart after seeing a Major get one for a small cut from a can of beans. The other men all agreed with me. This didn't make Capt. Happy very happy. He said I would have to appear before Gen. Leland for my attitude. When the General heard the whole story he laughed and agreed with me. I accepted the Purple Heart with honor, knowing that I had stood the test. Under great hardship I had not given in to the enemy. I knew the brothers would be proud of me. I was indeed a hero.

I was in the hospital for a total of 9 weeks. I wrote 2 letters to my wife explaining what had happened. The army offered to pay for her to come see me, but she declined the offer. I was given the choice to go home or go back to Nam. Well, I had one son I didn't even know, another baby on the way and a wife I really didn't care about, so I chose Nam. They asked me if I wanted to be a cook or an infantry officer. I said, "I want to go back to flying". But that was out of the question. As a result of my accident my vision had been impaired. I could never fly again. Well, I wasn't going to be no cook, so I chose the infantry. Back to combat, this time as a 1st Lieutenant.

◆ 16 ◆

Pride Before the Fall

I LANDED IN PHUI-CHUE (PHỦ Chủ?) and reported to the Company Commander, Capt. Linville. He welcomed me and offered me a chair. He stepped behind his desk and leaned forward. "I have some good news for you, son", he said. "You are the new Company Commander". "Excuse me, sir. Did you just say I am the Company Commander?" "That's right, son. I ship home tomorrow". He called for his aid to show me to my temporary quarters, I would be moving into the Command Tent the next day.

He shook my hand enthusiastically and dismissed me. I was now the Commander of the "Flying Eagles".

In my tent that night I was overtaken by the prospect of my own greatness. This could be the start of my revenge on the world and the people who had never given me a chance. After all I was a hero. The voice recorded in my subconscious tried to break through and force me back into the insecure existence I had known all my life. However, I pushed it back down and used the hatred to fuel the flame of my ambition. Anger and pride mingled together to form a resolve that would not be broken. I would show them all what I was capable of.

During this time I got a letter telling me that my wife was in danger of losing our second child. For some reason the news hurt me. I had pushed any thoughts of being a father down so deep I didn't realize they were there. When I heard that she might lose this one it brought it all to the surface. I did care. I wanted my child to live. There was no logical explanation for what I was feeling. I wanted my children to have a better life than I had. I wanted them to have a father. I continued to work, but I was totally distracted. A few days later I got word that he had been born prematurely. They were sending me home because I might have to take care of details.

I flew home and met my tiny son. I named him Wesley, after a famous race car driver in the 40's. I watched as he struggled for life. We almost lost him once. That was when I truly started to feel like a father. I wanted to breathe for him. I felt helpless watching his tiny chest move up and down fighting for each breath. He had needles and tubes tapcd to his little arms and legs and the diaper seemed to swallow him. My heart felt like it might burst with the thought of losing him.

While we were in the waiting area of the hospital one day my step-father talked to me. He made me promise I would stay married till the boys were 18. I wasn't sure I could live up to that promise, but I made it anyway. I would try at least.

Wesley pulled it off. He got stronger each day and soon they removed the breathing tube. He was breathing on his own! Then the IV's came out and he was sucking like a mad-man on the bottle the nurse gave him. The thought struck me, "Just like his old-man, sucking on the bottle". I chuckled to myself, but then it hit me, "I don't want my sons to have a drunk for a dad".

I went back to Nam with that ache still in my heart. I just couldn't shake it. I worked with a renewed determination pushing me from within. I just wanted to be the best I could be. I knew Alice would take good care of the boys and my mother helped out where she could. Alice went back to work and became head of the salad department then moved to the bakery where she made better money. I had always sent money to her from every pay check I got and the amount got bigger with each promotion.

I wrote a few times, mostly to mother. She told me the boys missed me. I couldn't understand how since they had hardly ever seen me. They were told that their daddy was a hero. Alice never once said anything bad about me to the boys, but her mother sure did. That woman hated me. With good reason, I might add, but injecting her venom into my boys was wrong. I tried to live up to the "hero" for my sons.

After just a few weeks I had made Captain. I was determined to go far. I started studying books about great military figures to become a better leader. Two of my favorites were Patton and Custer. I was especially fascinated with Custer. I found myself identifying with him and understanding his tactics. I got caught up the same way he did.

There were several minor skirmishes and we were on a winning streak. My pride continued to swell. I was sent orders to take hill 910. I was supposed to wait for Charlie Company to arrive so I could lead my troops up the front of the hill while Charlie Company took the rear. I saw an opportunity to make a name for myself and get promoted to Major at the same time. I saw visions of greatness. It was like a ticker-tape parade in my head. I also saw the faces of my relatives and teachers and others finally put in their places, realizing they had been wrong about me. I saw Jonny and Red and the other brothers riding in formation

Pride Before the Fall

behind me honoring the returned war hero. It was intoxicating.

I issued the order to take the hill. The men marched out before dawn. We began our ascent on the north face. The jungle was like a dense, dark maze making our progress slow and obstructing our view. The enemy came out of nowhere. Bullets pierced through the air ripping into bodies and tearing into flesh. Smoke filled the jungle and hovered among the trees. The sounds of exploding guns and dying screams were all around us. But my men were brave and well trained. We pushed ahead, guns blazing. Some were engaged in hand-to-hand combat. They fought fiercely. I saw a Vietnamese soldier decapitated with one swift cut from an army blade. He took five steps, still firing his weapon even though his head had been severed.

The battle lasted for an excruciating 20 hours. We reached the top of the hill

"Sprung From Hell"

and secured the area. We were victorious, but there were only 40 of us left. It had cost the lives of 149 American soldiers. I looked at the devastation around me. Bloody, broken bodies of men who had followed my order to march into battle without back-up were strewn over the hillside. Most of them had not even seen their 21st birthday. Every face flashed before my eyes in a single instant. I turned away from the gruesome scene and threw-up.

The next morning Charlie company arrived. We had begun the long process of retrieving the bodies of our dead and attending to the wounded. I could have been Court-marshaled for disobeying the order to wait, but because we were successful in taking the hill I got a slap on the wrist. I was reprimanded for my actions and denied the promotion to major.

I asked to be allowed to write the families of the men who had fallen. I thought it would help ease my conscience and stop the nightmares. It didn't, it only made it worse. I struggled to phrase the words in a way that would ease their suffering while trying to exonerate myself. All the while there was a terrible battle raging in my soul. Every time I closed my eyes their faces would parade through my subconscious. I searched for justification for my decision. I couldn't admit that I was wrong, that it was my selfish ambition that had caused the death of these good men. The weight of that guilt would crush me. I had to escape it.

There was nowhere for me to get alcohol, but I knew that opium was readily available. I had never done drugs before, but I had to find some way to make the turmoil in my mind go away, even if it was only for a little while. It wasn't difficult to find someone in the marketplace of a nearby village willing to sell me what I wanted. I learned to use a small piece of aluminum foil to heat it over a match or a candle then inhale the smoke through a straw. Opium burns very quickly so to expose it to an open flame wastes it. It is more potent if it is vaporized rather than burned. I became an expert at maintaining just the right temperature to get the most out of every bit.

Opium has been around for centuries and was used to relieve not only physical pain, but emotional too. It was the world's first antidepressant. It produced a gentle, subtle, dreamlike feeling of euphoria that I could not live without. My ambitions as well as my family were lost in the fog. Someone once likened opium to a woman, a beautiful and terrible lover, full of caresses and deceptions. I was completely bound in her arms. My addiction became so bad that I was sent back to the U.S. for treatment.

Well, I wasn't about to go to a rehab center and I couldn't go home, so I went

AWOL, and headed back to Oakland. I was a failure once more nothing mattered to me and so, I was prepared to party hard and live free and ride fast and pretend that nothing was wrong. I knew there was no hope for me, I was headed to hell, so I would go down partying.

A few days after I arrived, Madman decided I needed a real bike not my Frankenstein scooter. I don't know where he got it or who it belonged to, but I didn't care. Frankly I didn't care about much of anything except staying high and having fun.

Of course opium was not as easily obtained in the U.S. as it had been in Nam, but heroin was pretty easy to get if you knew where to go. Recreational drug use was a pretty common thing. It was part of life in the 60's. So, no one had a problem with my using at first. They welcomed me as a brother and I wore my colors with pride.

"Sprung From Hell"

We went to an open bar one night to celebrate my return. An open bar is a place where anyone can come in, unlike a biker bar. I was hustling pool when things got out of hand. I was playing with a big red-neck and he didn't like losing. He demanded that I give him his money back. I told him he was welcome to try and make me give it back. Well, he decided to leave and me and the brothers had a good laugh. But, about ten minutes later he showed up with four friends bent on teaching me a lesson. He sauntered up to me and punched me right in the nose and broke it. Blood was all over my face and I saw red alright. I started swinging with the pool cue and the whole place erupted into chaos. I don't remember much after that.

I came to my senses while riding back to the clubhouse. I don't even remember leaving or getting on my bike. It was like someone else took over my body for a while and I couldn't control what was happening. Hell, I don't even know what happened. When we arrived Doc asked if I was alright. "Course I'm alright, dammit", I cursed , "Why wouldn't I be?" He shook his head and said, "You are one crazy Indian!" Billy chimed in, "Yeah! You took everyone out including the bartender and the bouncer. I ain't never seen anyone as crazy as you". From that day on I was known as Crazy, and I lived up to it. I started trouble everywhere we went. I took to shooting people in the knee caps so I wouldn't have to fight.

One night I crashed and burned. I fell to the floor shaking all over and foaming at the mouth. Doc stayed by me all night and got me through it. The next morning he stripped my colors and told me if I wanted them back I'd have to get clean and prospect to get back in. I knew he was serious. I also knew I had to get my colors back. On my own I was nothing but a loser. The brotherhood was what gave me my place in this world. It was the only place I ever really belonged. Being a part of the club gave me my identity, without it I didn't know who I was.

I resolved to kick the drugs and do whatever I had to do to get my colors back. Doc helped me kick, cold turkey. It took two days to get all the heroin out of my system. It was excruciating. Pain wracked my whole body. Fever caused me to shake violently and attacked my mind with horrific hallucinations. I threw up everything in my stomach, but continued to heave for hours. When it was finally over I was too weak to even get up off the bathroom floor, so I slept in front of the toilet for a full day. When I woke up I felt a little better. I washed the vomit off myself and put on clean clothes. I found Hannah in the kitchen and she said, "Good you're awake, now you can clean up the mess you made".

Pride Before the Fall

"Yes ma'am", was all I said in reply. I turned to go back to the bedroom and start cleaning up. She stopped me and said, "I'm glad you're alright, sit down and eat something first. You'll need your strength".

Soon I was back on my bike. I asked what I had to do to prospect back in. They said I had to do clean-up jobs. That was something none of the brothers wanted to do. But I was desperate to get back in. There was no reason for me to live if I couldn't. Clean-up jobs meant just that, cleaning up loose ends for the club. I did three jobs and it started to get kinda hot. The cops were getting a little too close for comfort. Now, I had been AWOL all this time, but I decided it would be better to go back to Nam and face the military than to get busted by the authorities in the U.S.

I jumped a hop back to Nam and turned myself in to the new company commander of the unit. He said he didn't want to know what I had done just get back to work. I stayed straight and worked hard for him so I wouldn't get busted. Several months later I got word that my grandmother had died. I was shipped home for the funeral.

I showed up for the graveside service and stood back from the crowd. It wasn't easy for me to blend in though. I'm well over six feet tall and I was dressed in jeans and a white t-shirt with a leather vest and a bandana on my head, not exactly reverent funeral attire. It didn't help that I rode up late, on my Harley, which drew some attention. My uncles and aunts all but ignored me. My mother walked up to me and looked me up and down and said, "So, You're one of them now. Hmmm, I guess that's why you never bother to see your sons. Well, you always were a disappointment, guess nothing's changed". She turned and walked away.

Pride Before the Fall

I wish I could say I didn't care, that it didn't affect me at all, but truth is it stung all the way down to the place where the little boy inside me stayed hidden. I felt like I was 5 years old again a shameful, halfwit and I wanted to shrink away and hide so no one could see me. I walked back to my bike and revved the engine as loud as I could in an attempt to seem like I didn't need them or their approval and I roared out of the cemetery. I hadn't drunk in a long time, but it seemed a good time to start again.

Next morning I reported back to the base. They informed me I had been assigned to Ft. Sill. I was not happy about this arrangement and told the officer I preferred to return to Nam. He put in the request and within a few days I got new orders. I had to wait a few weeks before I would ship out, so I headed to Oakland.

Things were different now. I was treated like a newbie. Mums and a few others still hung around with me, but even that was different. I was terrified. I had no other family. If these guys rejected me I would be totally alone. It would mean my fears were real. I really was unlovable; broken, dirty, damaged, and deformed, a freak. So, I took another clean-up job in an effort to prove myself. I was going back to Nam anyway, so what did it matter. Jonny passed on his thanks through Mums, but I wasn't offered my colors back. I began to wonder if I would ever be accepted back in.

I arrived in Nam at the tail end of the conflict in 1972. From there I was going back to Germany. The military said I had to bring my family with me to keep my rank as captain. At first I wasn't real keen on the idea, but what my mother said at the funeral kept playing in my head. I had two sons. One I hadn't seen since he was four and the other since he was born. So, after considering it for a while I decided to give it a try.

I wrote to Alice asking if she would be willing to give it a chance and move to Germany with me. I never really expected her to say yes, but she did. Perhaps the prospect of a new country and a new life provided a glimmer of hope for her. Maybe she was just so tired of the life she had, any change would be welcome. I don't really know, but for whatever reason, we started making arrangements for family housing on the base in Germany. I was a trained military officer and a tough biker who had been in more fights than I could count and faced combat on the battle fields of Vietnam, but I was scared to death of two boys and a woman. What was I thinking?

I made a stop in Oakland before going home. Man had things changed! Our clubhouse had burned down and Jonny was in prison. He was still the president

"Sprung From Hell"

though and ran things from the inside. Doc was not doing well. They said he was dying. While I was there Madman laid his bike over and passed away from the injuries. We had a caravan for his funeral. Brothers from all over the U.S. showed up. Some other clubs came to show their support. It was the longest caravan I have ever been a part of. Since I was still considered a newbie I wasn't allowed in the pack. I rode behind the club members, but it was still an awe inspiring sight.

The service was a tribute to an honorable man who had been my friend. He would be missed by all. The party in his memory lasted for weeks. I enjoyed losing myself in the chaos for a while before life and duty demanded my attention.

I picked up my family and we flew to Charleston. I had a job to do for the club before leaving, so while the family waited in a hotel I met some of the brothers who put me on a small plane to N.Y. I was met there and given a bike and directions. I accomplished my task and was back in Charleston within 24 hours. Now we were off to a new country and a new life.

♦ 17 ♦

Germany and Fatherhood

ON THE PLANE RIDE TO GERMANY I finally took the time to really look at my sons. They seemed to have grown over night. Scott was almost 14 and Wesley was 11. I was shaken by how much of myself I saw in both of them. Scott had my dark hair and light, brown eyes. He was tall and well built. He actually looked more like Alice in the face, but he had my attitude and this fact showed in his mannerisms. There was no mistaking he was my son. Wesley looked more like me. He too had light, brown eyes but he had blonde hair like his mother. He was tall for his age too, but he had a quieter, more contemplative demeanor. He held his feelings deep inside where they simmered and stewed. Scott was more of an in-your-face kind. He had strong opinions and was not afraid to tell you exactly what he thought.

Neither of them had spoken to me since we left Oklahoma. I was a stranger to them who came and took them away from the only home they had ever known. I would catch them staring at me on occasion. I couldn't quite tell what they were thinking. Sometimes I thought I saw admiration, but mostly it seemed to be a mixture of fear and uncertainty.

I remembered being a boy and wishing that I had a dad. I remembered playing with the little blonde girl at the motel pretending that we were a happy family. I thought of watching "Leave it to Beaver" on TV and longing for a home like his. I wanted better for my sons. I wanted to be a man they could respect. I wanted them to be better than I was.

I didn't know that too much time had already been wasted. They had lived with much of the same abuse I had endured as a child. They were surrounded by poverty and despair. They were subjected to the hurtful words of the broken, insecure adults around them and beatings from a legalistic grandmother and an alcoholic grandfather. Their mother was too tired and caught up in her own pain to really care for them, so they were left to sort through the hurt and confusion and figure life out on their own. I learned later that Alice's brother had molested Scott. If I could have I would have gotten on a plane at that instant and gone home to kill him.

Germany and Fatherhood

They both had already been in trouble many times back home. It didn't take long before they were in it again. Calls from the school became an almost daily occurrence. I had good intentions, but not a clue how to actually live them out. I would get angry and yell at them, Alice would try to defend them and then I would fight with her and end up leaving to get drunk.

On top of the problems at home I found out upon my arrival in Germany that I could no longer be a Captain in my current position because that rank required administrative experience and I only had combat experience, so I was demoted to Buck Sergeant. I had to work my way up the ranks again.

Alice worked at the commissary because she wanted a distraction. The boys continued to grow up with no real direction. I proved to be a terrible role model. I was rarely home because

I preferred to avoid the conflict. When I was home I was usually drunk. Alice would assault me with criticism or problems with the boys as soon as I walked through the door. Her life had turned out to be no better in Germany than it had been in the U.S. and I was the source of her misery. I tried to get the boys in line the only way I knew how, yelling and hitting. It didn't take long for them to lose any respect they had for me.

I needed an escape from the stress at home and the frustration at work. I bought a BMW bike and joined the Autobahn Freedom Riders. Alice agreed because this was a way for us to avoid the luxury tax we would have had to pay for having two cars. With a bike and a car we weren't required to pay it.

On the outside we kept up the pretense of the happy military family. If I ever expected to get promoted I certainly couldn't let anyone find out that

Germany and Fatherhood

I was really an angry man with a severe drinking problem who had absolutely no control over his own life or his family's. Alice would have died if any of her friends found out what really went on behind closed doors. Her only reason for living was to hob-knob with the officer's wives and pretend that we had a story-book life. The boys complied in public probably because they were as embarrassed as we were about our home life, but the constant hypocrisy was taking a serious toll on their young minds.

The AFR too was a front. To the onlooker it seemed to be a very family oriented group. We had picnics and bar-B-Qs and took sightseeing trips to some of the castles and other sites in Europe. So, at least I can say I provided some culture and history for my sons. However, behind the sweet exterior the men knew how to party. The wives either didn't know or figured there was nothing they could do anyway, so we had our fun and continued the charade for our wives' benefit.

Meanwhile I put in for a promotion to Sgt. Major. I had to take a course in order to be eligible for the promotion and there were no slots available at the time. My name was added to the waiting list.

Later that year we received the news that Alice's father had passed away. We flew back to the States for the funeral. Alice's mom was beside herself. She draped herself over the coffin at the funeral and wailed, "Don't leave me, I don't want to live without you." Alice seemed irritated by her display, but attempted to comfort her anyway. Her mother never seemed to have much use for her husband while he was alive and now she was acting like he had been her reason for living. Maybe she was just upset not to have anyone to order around and to drag down into her own misery anymore.

Germany and Fatherhood

Well, while we were there a spot opened up in a Sgt. Major class. Alice said she and the boys would go back to live with her mother while I was in the class. Scott and Wesley were not excited about this, but like kids everywhere, they had no choice.

Their resentment toward me was growing stronger with each passing day. Looking back now I realize they wanted a relationship with me, but I was too busy searching for significance in my career. The substance of our relationships was conflict and pain. I was blind to the fact that I had become the abuser rather than the abused and my sons were carrying on the legacy of brokenness that was rampant in our family. They became increasingly more rebellious and Alice could no longer control them, so she gave up.

A little over a year passed and we were bound for Germany again. Scott was now almost 16 and Wesley 13. Scott had grown to be almost my height over that year and he had a temper to match his size. Wesley had become more sullen and closed off. There were nights when I would wake up from a drunken stupor and go to their rooms. I would watch them sleeping. They looked so young and vulnerable when they were asleep. Tears would flow as I grieved over my failure to show them that I really did love them. Why couldn't I be the man I wanted to be? I was still nothing but a half-wit. I destroyed everything good in my life.

Alice and I continued our fake life in public and grew more and more distant in private. Our fights had escalated and become more frequent and more violent. I was still a member of the AFR and stayed away from home as much as I could. The boys were not interested in any family outings by this time and Alice just put on more make-up and continued to pretend.

Germany and Fatherhood

When I was home you could cut the tension with a knife. I was drunk by 6:00 PM almost every night and my anger would flare with the slightest spark. Wesley came in one evening and headed straight for his room. I said, "Aren't you even gonna say 'hey' to your old-man?" He ignored me and just kept walking. I wouldn't have admitted it then, but I was hurt. I reacted out of that hurt the way I always did. I yelled and cussed at him, but he continued to ignore me. Now he was disrespecting me in my own house. I would not stand for that. I followed him to his room, removing my belt on the way, and grabbed him by the arm. He whirled around and yelled, "Let me go!" "You will not disrespect me, boy", I hissed through gritted teeth. I brought the belt down on his back over and over, unleashing my pent up frustration on him. He screamed for me to stop, but I was caught up in a blind rage and I didn't even hear him.

"Sprung From Hell"

Next thing I knew I was lying on the floor with a throbbing pain in my skull. I reached up to touch my head and felt a warm, sticky mess in my hair. I was bleeding. I tried to sit up, but the room was spinning out of control. I crawled to the phone and called the hospital.

This was certainly not the first time I had lost control. I had whipped both of the boys many times before, but this time Scott decided to do something about it. I don't know what he hit me with, but he had heard his little brother screaming and come in on the scene. He whacked me on the head and they both left in a hurry. I was in the hospital for four days.

We told people that I had tripped on a piece of loose carpet and hit my head on the coffee table. Everyone was very sympathetic. We never spoke of the incident within our family.

Time continued its relentless passing and we survived each day in tortured

Germany and Fatherhood

silence except when we were fighting. I became an MP and was training to be a criminal investigator with the CID.

Scott and Wesley stayed in trouble at school and elsewhere. They started sneaking out at night and hanging around at bars. There was no age restriction on drinking in Germany, so they could get whatever they wanted.

Scott got in a lot of fights and usually won, but Wesley held everything inside appearing to be calm on the outside. It took quite a bit of antagonizing to get him riled up, but once the damn broke he was a wild man. On one of these nights Wesley got into it with a German national and killed him.

The next day I heard about the incident at work. I knew somehow that my boys were involved. I confronted Scott because I figured it had been him. He stayed tight lipped and wouldn't tell me anything. As I was yelling and cussing at

Scott, Wesley came in and calmly stated that it had been him, not Scott who had killed the man.

I was shocked, not so much that Wesley had done it, I just figured the guy had pushed him too far, but at the callousness of his reaction toward what he had done. There was no remorse or any emotion at all. I guess I had passed on more of my attitude about life than I realized. I admit, part of me was proud of him, but part of me was frightened for him. I knew he would go to prison even though he was only 14. American prisons are one thing, but in a German prison I couldn't see him surviving.

I called Alice at work and told her to get home immediately. She wasn't happy about me ordering her home, but when she heard the situation she went into fix-it mode. "You have to get him out of the country right away", she commanded. I didn't even get mad at the way she was speaking to me because I knew she was right.

I arranged for the three of them to fly back to the U.S. that night. I stayed to finish out my tour. I went to the police academy and CID school trying to make something of myself again. It was all lost when the law figured out that I had blown their case by getting my son out of the country so fast.

My tour ended in 82 and I was assigned to Ft. Leonard wood in Missouri. Once again I was told it would look good if I had my family with me. They came shortly after I arrived. I started NCO school and took courses in administrative leadership. I made Master Sergeant and became a Drill Sergeant on the base. Even with all the training I had I still couldn't keep myself out of trouble. My sons hadn't changed either. They were following in my footsteps and heading straight for destruction.

◆ 18 ◆

Hit Rock Bottom

BY 1984 OUR FAMILY HAD ALL but fallen apart. Scott had dropped out of school and stayed gone most of the time. I don't really know what he was doing or where he was staying. He'd show up stoned out of his mind every once in a while asking for money. His mama would give it to him, which infuriated me. Wesley was constantly getting in fights at school.

One day in May I got a call from the principal saying that Wesley had been caught selling drugs on campus and he was expelled from school. I drove to pick him up mulling over in my mind what I would say to him. I knew this would be a defining moment in his life. I was determined to stay calm and try to talk some sense into him. I truly wanted him to have a better life than I had.

When I arrived he was waiting out in front of the school. He got into the truck without a word and slammed the door. He sat in defiant silence staring out the window for several minutes.

I struggled to control my temper and rallied up the courage to speak to him calmly. "Wesley, I don't want your life to turn out like mine", I started. "You need to finish school". "I'm not going back to school", he yelled. I could feel the anger rising up, but I forced it down and tried again. "I want you to have a better life than me". He turned to me with a cold stare and let loose of emotions he had stored up for years. "Why dad, because your life is so terrible? Because Scott and me ruined your life! Because mom was never good enough for you! Because you're nothing but a drunk and a loser and now your loser son has screwed up your plans again! Well, you can go to hell!"

I know now that he was crying out for help and for love from his father, but his cry was lost in the fog of my own pain. His words pierced through my resolve to stay calm and the rage boiled over. I back-handed him across the face and busted his lip. I screeched the truck to a halt on the side of the road and grabbed him by the front of his shirt. "You will either go back to school, get a job and start paying your own way, or get the hell out of my house, and don't ever come back!" "I like that last option", he gritted through his tears. He got out of the truck and slammed the door and ran off into a neighborhood next to the road.

Hit Rock Bottom

I pounded my fists on the steering wheel and punched the window beside me. The glass shattered and cut me in several places. I drove to the nearest bar oblivious to the blood dripping from my hand.

I didn't go home till about 2: AM. I walked into the silent house and went straight to Wesley's room. I sat there and cried like a baby till I passed out on the floor. I assume that Wesley must have called his mother because Alice never said a word to me about what had happened.

I had no idea where he was or what he was doing. I went through the motions at work and drank till I passed out at night. About two months later I got a call from the Sheriff's department. There had been an accident.

I arrived on the scene and saw a car literally wrapped around a tree. The headlight and the taillight were looking at each other and the passenger side of the car had been pushed to about twelve inches from the driver side door.

As I stood in stunned silence the Sheriff approached me. "Are you related to one of the occupants of the vehicle?" he asked. "I'm Kenner Weaver", I replied. "We believe your son may be the passenger sir". "What happened?" I inquired. "One of my officers was pursuing the vehicle because they attempted to run when the officer tried to pull them over for speeding. The driver hit this turn at about 126 Mph and lost control. We believe they attempted to escape because they had a large amount of marijuana in the trunk", he explained. "Uh, we will need you to identify the body sir", he stated apologetically.

I walked slowly up to the mass of tangled metal hoping that there was some mistake. My heart sank into my stomach when I saw Wesley's face smashed up against the windshield. His body was

Hit Rock Bottom

pushed up in front of the driver and the steering wheel was pressed almost through him.

The Sheriff informed me that he had been pronounced dead, but they needed my permission to use the jaws-of-life to get the other kid out. It would crush Wesley. I gave the okay and watched as they inserted the giant machine into the side of the car and began to pry it open. As the steering wheel moved slowly away from Wesley's chest I saw him suck in a breath. I thought I was hallucinating until I saw and heard him expel the breath. I screamed, "Stop! He's still alive!" I tried to run over to the men operating the machine, but two officers stopped me. I fought to get away until two more joined them in holding me back. I watched the jaws-of-life crush the life from my son's body.

I was engulfed in a wave of anger and grief, but instead of lashing out I fell to my knees beneath the great weight and watched as they removed my son's limp, lifeless body from the wreckage. My mind replayed the bitter scene from a few short months before. The last words he heard me say were, "Get the hell out of my house, and don't ever come back". The ache in my chest expanded to my whole body and I was rooted to the ground. The sirens screamed as if they felt my pain, as they rushed down the road to try and save the life of the person responsible for my boy's death.

The next day I had to go to the hospital to sign papers and I learned that the kid who had been driving the car was in a coma. I enquired as to which room he was in and went to see him. There was no one else in the room. He was lying on the bed with all sorts of tubes and contraptions attached to him. I didn't see a boy, all I saw was my son's murderer. I leaned down to his ear and whispered,

Hit Rock Bottom

"You better hope you don't ever come out of this coma, cause if you do, I'll kill you". The last I heard, he had gone crazy and was in an institution somewhere.

I wanted Wesley to be buried in Oklahoma, so it took every bit of money I had saved to pay for it. My life was on a downhill run and gaining momentum every day. I told myself I could hold it together, but I couldn't. Alice blamed me for Wesley's death and Scott was angrier than ever.

My current assignment ended and Alice wanted to go back to Oklahoma. I couldn't take it anymore. I told her I wanted a divorce. She agreed immediately. She left in Sept. and the divorce was final in Oct.

Scott paid me a visit in Oct. I was sitting alone in the dark nursing a glass of whiskey. He came in and just stood looking at me. It was eerie the way he was towering over me and not saying a word. After a few seconds I asked if he wanted something. "Just to make you pay for what you did to my baby brother", he growled. His voice sounded like something from the pits of hell. I realized he was high. It was then that I noticed he was holding something. It was a baseball bat and it was too late for me to react. He struck me on the head and I passed out cold.

I woke up in the hospital, once again. I don't know how I got there or how long I was passed out. Scott must have called the ambulance, at least that's what I told myself. He didn't want to kill me. He was just confused and angry over losing his little brother. The drugs made him do it. He wasn't in his right mind.

When I was released I found out that the commander had instituted a weigh-in program. I was told that I would not be eligible for any further promotions unless I lost weight. I tried, but with my

Hit Rock Bottom

drinking it proved impossible. I decided to request my retirement and just get out.

I was called into the commander's office for a "do better" talk. He said in no uncertain terms that I better lose weight or he would be forced to take action. I told him where he could put his action, because I was retiring in a month. He stood up and got in my face, so I hit him. Well, I retired a rank lower than I would have for that.

Meanwhile, Alice was trying to take me for everything I owned and then some. I hired the best lawyer I could afford. He did a good job, but even with that, alimony in Oklahoma is tough.

So, I had lost my son, Wesley, been beat with a baseball bat by my son, Scott, lost my marriage and my rank, all in the last six months. Now I was a civilian again. I was losing what little sanity I had left. I slipped into denial and reliance on the only coping mechanism I had; alcohol

"Sprung From Hell"

and drugs. But no matter how good you are at pushing things down deep in your subconscious they always come up eventually. It's like trying to hold a beach ball under water. Sooner or later it's gonna pop up. At that time however, denial was in full swing. I was sinking fast, but unwilling to admit it.

I rode from town to town like I had the world in my hand. For two years I outran my past. I left a wake of destruction in my path. I didn't know and convinced myself I didn't care where Scott was or what he was doing.

On the night of the two year anniversary of my discharge, I got a phone call. I was drunk and playing pool and enjoying the company of one of the dancers at a bar, so I didn't answer. The next day I listened to the message. Scott's voice came through. I could hear the desperation in his words. "Daddy, if you don't call back in fifteen minutes, I'm gonna blow my

Hit Rock Bottom

head off". I immediately called Mother. All she said was, "Come home".

I arrived later that day. I walked into the hospital to see Alice and all of her family and a lot of mine standing in the hall. Conversation came to an immediate halt and they all stared at me. I could feel as much as see the blame in their eyes. I had screwed up again. This time I knew they were right. My son had cried out for help and I let him down. It was my fault. Not only because I missed his call, but because I was a failure as a father. Hell! I was a failure as a human being. I didn't deserve to be loved. They were right! All along they had been right!

Mother pulled me away from everyone into an adjacent hallway. She asked if I would go in and identify him. She said the morgue would not release his body for burial until someone did. I felt as if I was drowning in the cesspool of my own worthlessness. Her words only partially registered in my chaotic mind. She led me by the arm to a cold, metal door with a sign that said, "Morgue". I shook my head as the realization hit of what I was about to do. Mother practically shoved me through the door. My subconscious took over and put up my armor in an effort to protect me from the sight.

"Are you Mr. Weaver?" the lab tech. asked. "Yes, I am", I answered with no emotion. "He's right over here, sir". I followed him to a table with a shrouded figure lying on it. He withdrew the cloth to reveal Scott's face. Most of the right side of his head was not there and his face was disfigured and badly bruised, but there was no question that it was Scott. I tried to keep my grief at bay, but it overcame me. I covered my face with my hands and wept. The lab tech. was sensitive enough to turn his back and leave me to say my goodbyes in privacy.

Hit Rock Bottom

I left the hospital without so much as a word to anyone.

I became "Crazy" the hardened biker again as soon as I mounted my ride. There was business to attend to. I called the brothers in California to ask if they would help me pay to bury my son. They said they would, but it meant another clean-up job for me.

Shortly after the funeral the call came with the instructions for the job. I was taken to a small town in Mexico where I met up with my contact to get the final details. The whole time I felt uneasy, of what I wasn't sure. It was like I too was being watched. On any job it was customary for there to be two other guys, one to watch your back and one to take over and finish the job if you couldn't, for some reason. A rooky may not have noticed, but I was no rooky, so I spotted at least three other guys in the

"Sprung From Hell"

vicinity hanging around trying to look inconspicuous.

I decided not to worry about them and just focus on getting the job done. After three days of waiting the opportunity came. I sprang into action, accomplished the task and disappeared into the crowd.

We left the next morning and rode hard till we were back in Texas. That is when I asked them why there had been so many guys. They looked at each other unsure of what to do. "What makes you think there were other guys?" one of them asked. I grabbed him by the neck of his dirty T-shirt and lifted him off the ground. "Listen, newbie, I don't have the name Crazy for no reason, so just answer the question", I demanded. They told me the extra brothers had been sent to make sure I didn't run out on the job.

If they had stabbed me in the gut it wouldn't have hurt as bad as those words

Hit Rock Bottom

did. It meant Jonny didn't trust me. I had never run out on a job. I had never given him any reason to not trust me. It was at that moment I truly gave up on ever getting my colors back. I dropped the guy in the dirt and rode off without a word.

I rode nomad after that. I had no desire to join any club, ever again. A couple of clubs asked me, but in my heart I was still loyal to my original colors and the betrayal was still too raw. Roy and I stayed friends and partied together. I made some new friends, Tenderfoot and Monroe. I moved to Houston for a while and stayed with Monroe and his old-lady.

I became a trucker while I was there. That worked for a while because I was always on the go. Running from my past, running from my pain and running from myself. When I moved to Ft. Worth and started working out of the office there it all came to an end. The boss was a cowboy named David and my biker lifestyle didn't fit with his plans. So, I was soon out looking for a new line of work.

I used my government training to get on as a game Ranger at Lake Whitney. I enjoyed being alone in the wilderness. I could lose myself in the quiet vastness around me. I never allowed my thoughts to wander into painful territory. I lived in a fantasy world where people didn't exist, only me and the trees and the birds and the animals. I was starting to lose my grip on reality. I loved to dive in the river, especially around the damn. There was always some treasure to be found. I started a little collection that I kept hidden in an old stump.

The Chief found out I could dive and wanted me to clean out the wind trips so the fans would work better. I told him I only dive for fun not for work. He said I could find other work then. So, I left my fantasy world and returned to the "real" world.

Hit Rock Bottom

I heard about a job with the Feds from a brother. Being an ex-MP and with my CID training I fit the job requirements. I became a Narc for the General Service Administration. (How weird is that?)

I was sent to Waco, Texas as an undercover officer. I operated a forklift in a warehouse where the feds suspected drugs were being shipped and sold. I fit in well with all the other workers and settled into a routine. As they began to trust me and let their guard down I noticed things that someone without my background may not have seen. I feigned disinterest while keeping my eyes and ears open.

A couple of lackeys had trouble keeping their mouths shut in the lunch room and I learned that it was the manager's son who was running the operation. These guys thought they were simply stealing a few wrenches and vice grips and selling them under the table.

They weren't aware of what else was in the crates of tools.

I passed on the information I gathered to my superiors. All the while I was working with the guys I was turning in. My dual life was getting to me. I was supposed to be one of the good guys, but I didn't even like my commander or any of the other stuffed shirts I worked for. I liked these guys. They were fun, down-to-earth, simple guys trying to make a living. "If the establishment treated them fairly and paid them what they were worth then they wouldn't need supplemental income", I rationalized.

With each passing day the line got more blurred. I started to be confused about who I was. My mind played a continuous loop of questions. "Am I a good guy or a bad guy? Are the drug dealers the bad guys or are the feds the bad guys? I'm one of them! I'm not a damn cop! What am I doing here? They're breaking the law,

Hit Rock Bottom

but they're my friends. It's my job, but I'm one of them!" I was drinking heavily and using prescription medications to dull my pain and spinning out of control.

The night came for the bust. I was there, but I was useless to the feds. I became disoriented not knowing which side I was on. One of my buddies looked me right in the eye asking, "Why?" just before he got shot. I watched him fall like it was in slow motion. I had to get out of there before I went crazy and killed them all.

I called in my resignation and started on a seven day binge. On the seventh day I received a phone call from my mother. She too was drunk and crying. "Kenner, this will be my last Christmas on this earth. You have to come home and see me now or you'll never see me again!" she sobbed. In my incoherent state I told her I'd come, mostly just to shut her up. I slept for several hours and woke up with a crick in my whole body and a pounding headache. Just as I reached for the bottle to have a little hair-of-the-dog I remembered the phone call. "Oh, crap! Guess I better go or she'll do something stupid, like show up at my door. I sure as hell don't need that". I took a long drink from the bottle and headed for the bathroom. I'm sure I smelled like death warmed over.

I took my supply of booze and pills, I knew I would need it, and hit the road. I intended to ride straight there say, "Hi", to my mama and start drinking hard and heavy. I didn't care much for Christmas, it held no good memories for me, and besides I figured God hated me and the feeling was mutual, so why should I celebrate His birthday? But I also knew if I didn't show up I'd never hear the end of it.

I made a detour to stop at my boys graves first. I'm not sure why. I grabbed the saddle bag from my bike which contained two bottles of whiskey and the prescription drugs. As I stood and looked at the two headstones the sky opened up and a torrential downpour soaked me to the skin almost instantly. At that very moment a damn broke in my soul. The rush of emotions that struck me in the gut was enough to knock me to my knees.

I saw myself as a tiny boy who no one wanted. I saw the small child confused by the world around him who just wanted a mom and dad to love him. I saw the preteen who was introduced to the possibility of revenge on those who had hurt him. I saw the young man who lashed out in anger and bitterness while the child within him was crippled with shame and self-hatred. I saw that child become trapped by the hardened man who abused his own wife and children and whose failure ultimately caused the death of his own sons.

The rain mingled with my tears and poured out to form the pit of utter hopelessness that was sucking me down into the graves that held my boys. My heart was gripped in a vice of fear at the prospect of facing the God who had never loved me and who had abandoned me the day I was born. I shook my fist and screamed into the dark night, "I hate You!"

I sat there for hours until I collapsed in the mud next to the two empty, whiskey bottles and the grave stones of my boys. When I came to it was still dark. I never went to Mother's. I rode back to Texas. I stopped on the way to buy two six packs and went to a favorite fishing spot of mine. I don't know how long I sat there staring out at the water. I took several pills and finished the beer. The air was frigid and the sky tormented me, alternating between pouring rain, icy sleet and freezing snow.

It was Christmas Day, 1987 and I was sitting on a rock looking out over Texas Lake with my life in a crumbled, decaying mass at my feet. For some reason I decided to go for a swim. I don't know if I was actually hoping I would die or if I just didn't care if I did. I stripped off my clothes and dove into the icy waves. My tortured mind did not even register the shock of the cold water as I sank into its depths. Numbness spread through my body. I surrendered to the will of whatever forces were controlling my destiny and floated to the surface.

Off in the distance, breaking through the mist, I saw a dark shape approaching me. As it got closer I recognized the hull of a small boat. There were two men rowing toward me. Fishermen, I assumed. "Why would anybody, in their right mind, be fishing on a night like this?" I thought to myself. I began to feel a sense of foreboding creep up my spine. I swam for the shore.

I climbed onto a pile of rocks and watched with dread as they continued their approach. They pushed the boat on to the shore and began to pull on their net, unloading what appeared to be a large catch. "Looks like you got a big haul", I said, trying to shake the ghostly feel of the scene. They worked in silence, not even acknowledging my presence. I walked a little closer asking, "What did you catch?" Again, I was met with silence. I walked closer and saw that it was a body tangled in their net. "You need to leave that body alone", I warned. They ignored me and continued trying to free their nets from around its lifeless limbs. The mist from the lake swirled around them and the steam from my own gasping breath added to the nightmarish feel of the night. I cautiously stepped closer and peered down into my own face. The body was me!

I woke the next day in a stark, white room with bright lights piercing my eyes. My arms and legs were fastened to the bed with leather straps and there were tubes protruding from various places on my body. A petite lady in a white uniform and cap said, "Welcome to Terrell County Mental Institution". I struggled to free myself from my restraints. "I'm not crazy!" I tried to yell, but only garbled mumbling sounds would come out. She shushed me and stuck a needle in my arm. "Don't worry, we have a place for you", she soothed. I slipped into blackness. I had truly hit rock bottom.

♦ 19 ♦

Punching God in the Face

I WAS DIAGNOSED AS A COMBAT veteran with post traumatic stress disorder. I was a prisoner once again and the state had complete control of my future. I was kept pretty well sedated all the time. I gave up and retreated within myself. The days ran into each other with a mundane rhythm of group sessions, meal times and free time in the game room. I started playing chess with one of the interns and we became friends.

One evening I beat him four times in a row and he said, "You don't need to be in here. You're as sane as me". I laughed because I thought he was just sore about losing. "I'm serious", he said, "I want to help you get out".

The next day a new doctor came to see me. He asked a lot of questions. He determined that the only problem I had was addiction and if I dealt with that I'd be okay. He had me transferred to a treatment center where I was detoxed from all the prescriptions I had been taking. I was there for forty-eight days.

The doc came to see me again and declared me cured. He said I would be released if I promised to join an A.A. group or an N.A. group immediately. He said he'd be keeping tabs on me and if I missed the meetings he'd put me right back in Terrell County. I promised that I would be faithful.

"Sprung From Hell"

I moved back to Ft. Worth and got a job as a forklift driver. I took my time looking for a group to join (like not at all) till I got the first "check-up" call from the doc. He gave me the number to call so I figured I was stuck.

As soon as I walked in to the meeting hall a big cowboy grabbed me by the shoulder and said, "Outside". I was accustomed to being unwelcome in certain settings, so it didn't really surprise me. Most people get pretty uncomfortable when a 6'4" guy with long hair and a braided goatee dressed in leather roars up on a Harley. I said, "You're on!" and walked out prepared to fight.

I faced him, waiting for him to make the first move, when he simply stated, "You're a Vet". A bit confused, I replied, "Yes, I am. What's it to you?" "What unit?" he asked. I began to list off some of my units and before long we were sharing war stories. After a few laughs he said,

"I can help you, if you're ready". Well, I wasn't sure I was ready, but I didn't want to go back to Terrell, so I said, "okay".

I started attending the meetings, but I didn't think it applied to me. Those people were alcoholics and drug addicts, I wasn't, and any time they started to pray or talk about God I just left.

Cowboy and I started meeting on a daily basis. Every day he would start by taking my weapons and then we would talk about Vietnam. We formed a bond of respect and trust. I had begun to make some progress dealing with the things that had happened in Nam. I gained some insight and understanding about the recurring nightmares I was plagued with. He helped me face some of the hard realities and the dreams had become fewer and further between.

A couple of months passed and Cowboy got sick. He told me to look up another man who would help me continue to heal. I took the number, but I didn't call, because I refused to admit that I was losing him. After he died I

"Sprung From Hell"

was furious. I needed him and that only pissed me off more. I was helpless and there was nothing I could do about it. He was gone. God had screwed me again and I couldn't even hit Him.

About a week later I was sitting on the steps of my apartment building feeling trapped by my own existence when a big, black man in a trench coat walked up and just watched me. I began to feel uneasy and stood up to confront him. Before I could say anything, he questioned, "Why didn't you call me like you were asked to?" I knew then who he was, the man Cowboy told me to call. I looked him over assessing in my mind what kind of man he might be. He met my gaze without a flinch. His eyes were almost cold, like a killer, but there was more there and I decided to trust him, for Cowboy's sake.

Blackie and I started our journey together that day. He said I needed to work through the twelve steps. I was an addict, he said, and until I faced that fact I would not be able to move on. I was not keen on that idea, but Terrell County Institution was still a threat, so step one here I come.

Admitting that I had a problem that I was powerless to control on my own proved to be a huge step for me. If I admitted my powerlessness that would mean something else had power over me. Everything within me rebelled against this notion. Blackie worked long and hard to break through my pride and fear.

One night, at a meeting, there was a guest speaker. I listened as this man told his story and felt as if he had been watching my life and was telling about me. After the meeting I went up to him and asked him how he knew he had a problem. He looked at me and I swear he could see into my soul. He asked me, "Who has been controlling your life up to this point?" "I have", I stated matter-of-factly. "How's that working out for you?" he inquired. I was dumbfounded. I had no response. He patted me on the shoulder and walked away silently. I left the hall that night knowing that I had a problem and I was powerless to handle it on my own.

Step two; admitting that there is a God and He wants to help me. This was not happening. I did not believe in God! I had convinced myself that I was an atheist. Of course, logically speaking, I could not be an atheist since I hated God and you can't hate something you believe does not exist, but I was not thinking logically at the time.

There were two other members of the group who claimed to be atheists. One of them had fifteen years sober and the other twenty-two, so I asked them how they got past this step. They explained that "God" was merely a term used to describe a higher power. Each person's higher power is different they rationalized. You have to discover what yours is. Perhaps it is simply the strength down deep in your soul that you have not tapped into yet. Honestly, this seemed a little hokey to me, but if it worked, oh well.

Step three; turn my life and my will over to "God". Okay, so if "God" is the strength deep down in my soul that I haven't discovered yet and I'm supposed to turn my life and my will over to "Him", how does that fit with admitting that I am powerless to do this on my own in step one? I was so conflicted. I just couldn't accept it. Of course I had not really completed step two so I was at an impasse. All I knew to do was just make it to the meetings. Sometimes I would go to as many as four a day. I didn't want to drink, I knew that.

Blackie could see the turmoil in me. He told me to go to church and find God because He was the one I was really mad at. Go to church! Oh that was a good one! "Okay, I will!" I stated spitefully.

I decided to find the biggest, fanciest church in town and ride my bike right up the middle of their manicured lawn and park on their ornate front steps. The First Methodist Church seemed to fit the bill. Sunday morning I did just that. I wish I had it on film. It was like a scene from a cheesy, horror flick, women gasping and men shuffling their families out of harm's way. The personification of evil had descended on them and they were appalled.

I screeched to a halt right in front of their doors and cut the engine. I scanned my surroundings and saw some people actually hiding, others staring in amazement, mothers covering their children's eyes. I was enjoying this, a lot! A young boy started to walk up to me exclaiming, "Cool bike!" only to be grabbed by his father and told to stay away from me.

That irritated me. I got off the bike and started to walk towards the door.

I was intercepted by two men trying their hardest to look tough; though I'm pretty sure I could see their knees shaking. "I'm afraid we're going to have to ask you to leave or we'll call the police", one of them stammered. "I came here to find God", I explained. "Well, you'll have to look elsewhere sir, we don't want you here. Please leave or I will call the police." "Humph, doesn't surprise me", I replied, "If I was Him I wouldn't want to go here either". I fired up the engine and revved it a few times, gave a thumbs-up to the little boy still staring admiringly at my bike and left a thick, black patch of rubber on the polished porch as I peeled away.

I reported to Blackie that I had gone to church and God was not there. He said to try again. So, the next Sunday I tried my luck with the Presbyterians. It was

"Sprung From Hell"

pretty much the same deal. Blackie said, "Don't give up".

Monday at work I shared my experience with one of the guys. He said, "Come to my church". I laughed and said, "Oh, I can see that going over well, me, the only white boy in an all-black church". "Just give it a chance", he challenged. I agreed, "Alright, I will", with some hesitation.

On Sunday morning I pulled my bike up on their front porch. This time they invited me in. A polite young man asked if I would like him to help me find a seat. I allowed myself to be led to the front row without protest because I was in shock at how I was being openly accepted.

The choir filed onto the stage and the music started. Everyone sang at the top of their voices. The choir swayed and clapped in perfect unison. The volume swelled and people began to shout and dance and some ran up and down the aisles with hands raised to the ceiling. I just knew they had a bottle of the good stuff stashed somewhere. The celebration continued for some time. I watched in amazement. The joy and excitement they displayed was somehow pure and more real than anything I had ever experienced before. I wished I had something in my life to be that happy about.

The preacher stood and walked to the center of the stage. The congregation quieted and took their seats. He was a small man, probably in his late sixties maybe early seventies, with black peppered through his gray hair. He wore wire rimmed glasses and had a short beard with the same touch of gray as his hair. There was nothing intimidating about him at all, but he stood with an air of authority and confidence. When he spoke it was with a passion and fierceness that reached out and grabbed me.

He told a story about a father who watched and waited daily for the return

"Sprung From Hell"

of a son who had turned his back on him. The son had really made a mess of his life and when he hit the bottom he decided to go home and offer himself as a servant to his father knowing that he no longer deserved to be his son. When the father saw his son coming in the distance he ran to meet him and restored him as his son without even a question.

Throughout the message there were periodic, heartfelt cries of "Amen" or "Preach, brother" or "Glory". I began to feel an ache in my chest. The preacher's words were hitting a little too close for comfort. I started looking for a way out, but I was on the front row. Why had I let that kid sit me right in the front? I tried to ignore the uneasiness that was creeping through my body and just hang on till it was over so I could make a quick exit.

The preacher said, "Amen" and people started moving from their seats. This was my chance. I stood to leave and suddenly the preacher was right in front of me. He looked up at me and said, "You don't believe in God, do you?" "How in the hell do you know that?" I asked. He just continued to look at me knowingly and said, "You're in recovery from drugs and alcohol too". Again, I asked, "How do you know that?" He didn't answer; he just kept looking at me. I began to feel very uncomfortable. Then he said, "You want to talk to God, don't you?" Normally I would have laughed at that question, but he was serious and so I said, "Yes, I do", wondering what his response would be. He instructed me to come back the next morning and he would introduce me to Him.

I went back to see how this preacher was going to introduce me to God and because I had a thing or two to say to God. I entered the church and walked slowly to the front. There were several old folks sitting together praying. I felt a sense of reverence and sat down quietly trying not to disturb them. After a few seconds the Pastor approached me. I stood up not knowing what to expect and waited for him to speak.

He gazed intently into my eyes and said, "Kenner, I am God's transmitter. I want you to say or do to me what you would say or do to God". I hesitated for only a moment, and then I hit him in the face. I was actually embarrassed and shocked that I had hit a little, old man, but it had been a split second reaction to the thought of how I felt about God. I didn't even realize how intense my anger was toward Him.

The preacher stood slowly and wiped blood from his mouth. He faced me once again and said, "Kenner, I am God's transmitter. I want you to say or do to me what you would say or do to God". The flare of rage I experienced was so sudden it scared me. I hit him again, harder this time. It took me a few seconds to collect my emotions and when I did I saw the preacher struggling up from the floor. His hand slipped in the blood on the polished tiles and he almost fell again. He turned to me with tears in his eyes and blood all over his wrinkled face from his now broken nose and said, "Kenner, I am God's transmitter. I want you to say or do to me what you would say or do to God". I drew back to hit him again, but my hand wouldn't move. It was like it was being held back by some unseen force.

There was a light coming from his face. It got brighter and brighter till all I could see were his eyes. The pure understanding and acceptance radiating from them started to melt my heart. I was crushed with the realization of my own sin and how I had hurt Him by pushing Him away for so long. The power of His unconditional love for me smashed into the wall that had been standing deep inside me since I was a child. My life flashed before me like a streak of lightening across the night sky. In that moment God communicated His heart to me.

I dropped my arm and asked, "Why are you doing this?" He answered, "Because my Lord loves you and I can do no less". I sank to the floor in complete surrender. He reached his hand out to me and introduced himself. "I am Pastor Smith; it's nice to meet you." I stared at his hand, smeared with his own blood, and was overcome with gratitude for the grace he was extending to me. I reached out and took his frail hand. Through that simple act I accepted whatever God had for me.

One of the ladies who had been praying brought a clean towel for the pastor and then began wiping the floor where his blood had been spilled. Every one of them had sat quietly, praying and watching as their pastor offered himself as a representative of the God they served. Each one stood reverently and left without speaking a word. We sat down on the front row in that tiny church and Pastor Smith walked me through my salvation experience.

He explained how every person, since Adam and Eve, was born infected by a disease called sin. (Rom. 3:23)This disease ravaged lives and destroyed people. God, in His love, wanted to save us, but the only way was by paying the awful price that holiness demanded. (Heb. 9:22) A perfect sacrifice had to be made. God offered His only Son as that sacrifice. "Jesus endured the torture of the cross because of the joy that was set before Him." (Heb. 12:2) We were that joy and I was a part of it. Now we have been given the opportunity to become children of God and heirs of eternal life, if we receive Him and believe in our hearts and confess with our mouths that Jesus is our Lord. (Titus 3:4-7, John 1:12, Rom. 10:9-10)

Hours passed as we talked and prayed. I was soaking up the words of the God I had rejected and misunderstood all my life. As Pastor Smith patiently taught me from the pages of the Bible I began to understand some of the happiness I had witnessed in the church service the day before. I was gently reminded of how many times I had broken God's law and I knew that I deserved to be punished, but Jesus had taken the punishment for me. I left that afternoon feeling like a different person. I was lighter, somehow. Every time I thought of the gift I had been given, though I didn't deserve it at all, I experienced a new surge of hope.

I called Blackie and practically yelled over the phone, "I found God!" "Did you hurt him?" he laughed. "Well, actually I kinda did", I muttered. "What? Tell me what happened", he burst out. I relayed the whole story to him. He listened attentively and voiced his approval of my decision with sincerity.

"Now we can get on with the steps", he declared. "No, Blackie, I've got to learn everything I can about God. I've given my life to Him and now I'm gonna work for Him". "Kenner, you need to finish the steps," he said emphatically. "No, I've made up my mind. I'm going to Bible college", I stated. He knew there was no arguing with me once I had made a decision, so he just said, "Alright, I'm always here for you, man". The next day I enrolled in Kenneth Copeland College. It was Dec. of 1988. Classes started in Jan. for mid-semester. I was on my way to a whole new life.

◆ 20 ◆

Beauty From Ashes

I ATTACKED MY STUDIES LIKE A starving man would attack a steak dinner. I couldn't get enough. I went to Bible study after Bible study. I learned about doctrine and theology and a lot of other big words that were all new to me. I read everything I could get my hands on that had to do with my new faith. With every new discovery I was convicted again about my life and felt renewed joy and gratitude for the gift of forgiveness.

Surprisingly, I got along with everyone. The professors admired my eagerness and my excitement about new concepts. My fellow students, who were all quite a bit younger than me, respected my age and experience and were intrigued by my past. I was encouraged by their youthful enthusiasm.

About six months after I started classes some students decided to try doing some prison ministry. They asked me to join them. I was flattered that they wanted me to be a part of their plans, so I accepted the offer willingly.

I pictured a large group of inmates moved to repentance by the telling of my story. It would be so amazing to watch them all coming forward for prayer, laying their hurts and fears at the foot of the cross and receiving the gift of grace that would change their lives forever. Surely this was why God had called me. I couldn't wait till the day arrived. I was full of vim and vigor and ready to conquer Satan on his own turf.

We arrived at Palestine Prison and were escorted through the many gates and locked doors. Each time I heard a gate close behind me and the locks grind into place I felt fear closing in. This was too soon. Who did I think I was that I could preach to the inmates? I was no better than them. I told our team leader I was not ready to speak in front of the crowd and he said he understood. I sat off to the side during the music and preaching. I looked at the faces of the men in the audience. Most were there just to break up the monotony of their days. They were not really interested in what was being said. As a matter of fact they probably resented these "church people" coming in to tell them they needed God. I remembered my own attitude toward anything having to do with God and I was overcome with discouragement.

When the service was over I was asked if I would talk with one of the prisoners.

He had requested to speak with someone from our group. I agreed, thinking that maybe I would do better one-on-one.

I was taken to one of the visitation rooms and a guard entered with a man dressed in a gray prison jumpsuit with hand cuffs on his wrists. He was only about 5'10" and couldn't have weighed more than 165 lbs. I relaxed a bit, feeling like I had the upper hand. That was my old way of thinking. Sizing a man up by his physical appearance and whether or not he posed a threat to me. The guard removed the man's cuffs and then moved quietly to stand outside the door. I extended my hand and said, "I'm Kenner, I'm pleased to meet you". He looked at my outstretched hand and ignored the gesture. He pulled a chair out from the metal table in the center of the room and sat down. I suppressed the desire to lift him up out of the chair and throw him against the wall. That was the old Kenner,

I was different now. I pulled the other chair out nonchalantly and sat facing him.

He continued to stare at me and didn't say a word. I started to feel a little nervous, like I was on the spot. I needed to say something that would crack his tough exterior so God could get in. I know now that my mistake was thinking that I could do anything to "help" God out. I was acting in pride and didn't even realize it. My Lord was at work, but I was the student, not the inmate I was speaking to. I stammered around for a few seconds and then blurted out, "God loves you!"

You could have cut the tension in that room with a knife. The look that began to spread across his features was dark and vicious. He stood slowly and walked around the table, never taking his eyes off me. I stood up abruptly, knocking my chair over. This little guy, who I had seen as no threat, grabbed me by the collar and actually lifted me off the floor

Beauty From Ashes

and slammed me into the wall. His eyes seemed to radiate pure evil as he glared at me and snarled, "If you got God in you, get him out, 'cause I want to see him". I was so shocked I didn't know how to respond. It was like the devil himself was challenging me and I was helpless in his grasp.

The guard must have heard the metal chair crash against the concrete floor. Before I knew it several armed men had come in and subdued the prisoner. As they dragged him from the room he kept his eyes riveted on me daring me to make a stand.

I left there that day with a hole the size of Texas in my heart. I started replaying old thoughts. "You dumb half-wit! How could you just stand there?" "You have failed again and this time you failed God!" "Is there no hope for you?" I went to talk with the dean. He said the way I was feeling was normal. I just needed to read the Bible more.

I doubled the time I was spending each night in reading the Word. I searched the pages for an answer to the emptiness I was experiencing. I read in Matthew about Jesus being baptized. That was it! I had never been baptized. I just knew that was the answer. God was not pleased with me because I had not followed His example. Surely, if Jesus had to be baptized, I did too.

The next morning I was waiting at the dean's door when he arrived. "Good morning Kenner, is there something I can help you with?" he inquired. "I need to get baptized", I responded. "Oh, I see. Well, that certainly is a fine thing to do. We will be having baptisms in June", he offered. "No, I need to be baptized now!" I demanded. He looked a little shocked at my fervency, so I softened my tone and pleaded, "Please sir, it's very important to

Beauty From Ashes

me". "Well, I suppose you could go to the little church in town and ask them if they will baptize you sooner", he suggested. "Thank you", I yelled over my shoulder as I ran towards the road.

It was a few miles to the town, but I ran all the way. Out of breath and sweating from the exertion I entered the quaint church office and asked to speak with the pastor. The receptionist gave me a cup of water and went to tell the pastor I was there. He informed me that they were performing baptisms the next week and I was welcome.

That week felt like an eternity, but the day finally arrived. I showed up early, towel in hand, ready to be dunked. The receptionist, who had been so kind to me the week before, giggled at my anticipation as she took down my name for the certificate.

I stepped into the cold water and shivered slightly, maybe from the temperature maybe from excitement. The pastor asked me if I had received Jesus Christ as my Lord and Savior and I answered enthusiastically, "Yes!" He covered my mouth and nose with his hand and lowered me into the cool water. It washed over my parched soul and refreshed my thirsty spirit. As I came up out of the water I saw my Lord standing in front of me and He said, "It's going to be alright, Kenner".

The "high" I was on lasted for a few weeks. I carried my certificate around with me and showed it to everyone. It didn't take long for people to get annoyed with me. I began to feel there was still something wrong. I wasn't sure if something was missing or out of place or what. The old recordings were still playing in my head and I didn't know how to make them stop.

I went to the dean again and he dismissed my problem as something that would pass in time. I sought out my class leader. He said it was all in my head and I just needed to study harder and focus on my goals. I tried, I really did, but it only seemed to get worse.

At the end of my rope and not knowing where else to turn, I called Blackie. He said he knew what I needed and to come home. I left the next day. I didn't even tell anyone I was going.

It was good to see my friend again. It truly felt like I was home. There was also some bad news. Blackie was very sick. The doctors had given him only a few months to live. He wanted his last act of ministry on this earth to be helping me. He explained that although I had received forgiveness at the moment I trusted Jesus, receiving healing was a process that would take some time. I told about being baptized. He said, "That was a good thing you did. We should always obey the Lord, no matter what, but you may have done it with the wrong understanding of why. Nothing you do can cause God to love you less and nothing you do can cause Him to love you more. He just loves you!" As that truth seeped slowly into my heart I was astounded by His love. Nobody had ever loved me like that. It would take some time for that belief to truly become a reality in my life. I moved in with Blackie and we picked up on step three where I had left off in my recovery.

Step three is turning your life over to God and believing He will help you. I had gotten stuck on this last time, but now I believed God loved me and so I turned my life and my will over to Him.

Step four is a very difficult step. It is where you are asked to take a moral inventory of yourself. This includes harm you have done to others, harm that has been done to you for which you are harboring resentment, and faults or shortcomings you see in yourself. Needless to say, my list was long. It was one of the hardest things I've ever done. I cried so much I looked like I'd been beat up. I listed a few people and events from my childhood, I listed things I had done to others while growing up, I listed things I was involved in while I had my colors, I wrote a little about Vietnam and then I came to my shame and guilt over my son's deaths.

I labored through the task and tried to separate myself from the crushing weight. I wrote as if I was writing about someone else. Surely this stubborn, selfish, cruel person could not be me. Blackie encouraged me through the whole excruciating process and finally I was done, at least as done as I could be. There were many things that still needed to be dealt with, but the Lord is patient with His children, so He allowed me to tackle only what I could handle at the time.

The next step, step five; is confessing your guilt to God, yourself and others. Confessing to God was okay, because He knew it all already anyway. Confessing to myself, well I knew I was a screw-up and a failure so I admitted that fact to myself pretty readily.

But sitting in the group, with others listening intently to my every word, with looks of sympathy on their faces, made something snap inside me. I was angry with them for feeling sorry for me. I was a worse sinner than any of those panty-wastes had ever dreamed of being. I stood and shouted at the whole lot of them, "You people don't know the first thing about guilt! You want to know about guilt? Let me tell you a thing or two." I started spilling my guts all over the floor. They all listened patiently, though there was an occasional gasp or look of shock.

When I finished the room was dead silent. I started to feel exposed, like I was on display. I had just bared my shame in front of all these people. I was about to run, when one person started clapping. Soon the whole room erupted with applause. Blackie came over to me and hugged me. "You did it!" he said, "I'm proud of you".

We all sat down and our leader got up to speak. "Thank you all for your honesty", he began. "Now we are going to talk about forgiveness". He spoke of how much God loves us. So much that He gave His all to have a relationship with us. He also taught us that we don't have the right to sit in the judge's seat, only God has that right. Only God is truly just in His judgment. God has declared us righteous because of His Son, Jesus. We no longer have the right to pass judgment on ourselves or others. This concept messed me up!

After the meeting I went to talk to him. "How can I forgive myself when I

"Sprung From Hell"

know it was my fault?" I asked. "I never said it wasn't your fault", he replied, "I said, God has declared you 'not guilty', because of Jesus, not because of you". He let that thought sink in for a second, then said, "Neither am I saying that what people did to you wasn't their fault. Only God has the right to judge them, not you. You need to forgive them, meaning take yourself out of the judge's seat and let Him do His work".

That night I took my inventory sheets out into the alley and made a fire in an old trash can with them. As I watched the smoke float up towards heaven I imagined my burden being carried there too. I prayed and gave thanks for the amazing gift of forgiveness that had been given to me and I forgave the people of the past, including myself. I watched the papers curl and turn to ashes and thought how my old life was like those papers, gone. A sudden gust of wind rushed down the alley and took with it the smoke and the ashes leaving a beautiful trail of sparks. I heard my Lord say, "I will bring beauty from the ashes".

◆ 21 ◆
Birth of a Ministry

I CONTINUED TO WORK THE steps and gained more and more freedom as time went on. When step nine came along, which is making amends to people you have hurt, I was in a much better place in my heart and in my life. I wrote letters apologizing to many of them, some alive and some passed on. It was very freeing.

I guess God decided I was ready for a little test. He was calling me to venture into an area of ministry that had never been done before, but I didn't know that yet.

Birth of a Ministry

I had gone to a biker bar to visit with some friends, Trucker and Brownie. We were sitting at a table drinking soda and laughing about one of Trucker's adventures when Gunny came through the door with three other guys from my old life. He was a long time member of Jonny's club. He knew me and he knew my past. I felt a wave of cold, like death had swept into the room. I knew he was there to see me. I told Trucker and Brownie to contact my father if anything happened to me so he could take care of arrangements. They looked at me with understanding and moved away from the table without saying a word.

Gunny sauntered up to my table and took a seat. The others stood behind him with their arms crossed like body guards. Gunny sure didn't need a body guard though. He barked for the waitress to bring him a whiskey, straight and then glared at me. "You drinkin sodie pop now?" he mocked. "Yea I am, a lot has changed for me", I stated. "Like what?" he challenged.

I began to relate the story of how God had worked in my life. I couldn't really tell you exactly what I said because the Lord visited us and He spoke through me. Words would come out of my mouth and I would think, "Wow! that was good. Did I just say that?" I know I told him about A.A. and how I was now working with others to help them progress through their healing from addiction.

I finished my account and sat back to wait for the verdict. Time crept along with them staring at me and me staring back at them. I wasn't about to back down. I was a Christian now, but I wasn't a coward. After several seconds Gunny said, "Buy us a beer". I knew then that all was well. They drank their beers and asked me a few more questions. Gunny

Birth of a Ministry

asked for my number and told me he would pass on word to Jonny that I was okay. Turned out Jonny had sent them to check on me because he was worried. I knew there was more to it, but I also knew it was best left alone.

I prayed that the Lord would speak to them and draw them to Himself. I was glad for the chance to tell some of my old brothers what God had done for me. That encounter planted a seed in my heart that I was not even aware of.

I worked hard for A.A. I led meetings and sponsored several people. I was speaking at meetings and churches all over town. I was offered a position as an associate pastor for Grace Country Cowboy Church. I accepted and was ordained as a minister. I enjoyed my time there and met some very special people, but the seed God had planted in my heart was starting to sprout and move into my brain.

"Sprung From Hell"

I was still a biker to my core. I had an ache in my spirit for my brothers who needed to hear the good news that God loved them and forgiveness was available to them, but I knew they would never listen unless it was delivered in a specific way, the biker way, and there was no one I knew of who was doing that.

I heard about the C.M.A. (Christian Motorcycle Association) and thought maybe this was the answer. I went to a rally in Oklahoma. For the most part I didn't see any hardcore bikers. I asked around for information and learned of the Bikers for Christ in Bowie, Tx. I contacted them and requested a charter to start a chapter in Ft. Worth. They granted it without any question.

I found that it was not easy to get a Christian biker organization going. The Christian guys who were interested were just weekend riders not experienced with biker culture and any seasoned

Birth of a Ministry

riders were not keen on the whole Christian thing.

I gave up and went back to the C.M.A. I asked how I could get a true biker club started with Christians. They insisted that I needed to join their organization. I declined their invitation and decided to try another Christian group in Ft. Worth.

It wasn't a true club, but they were involved with the community in several ministries and I liked that. However, when one of the members found out that I had been a member of an outlaw, one-percenter club in the past they kicked me out. Guess I tainted their spotless image.

Somehow the Tarrant County Baptist Assoc. found out about my desire to start a Christian club. They said they would sponsor it. I went to the C.M.A. and they sanctioned it. That is how "God loves Bikers Too" was started. Many of my friends wanted to be a part of it, so we started a Biker Church. Four other Christian groups joined us and I had hopes of equipping some of our members to reach bikers with the truth eventually.

It seemed to be going well until one Sunday when I invited a black preacher to speak to our congregation. The owner of the building and some of our members didn't like that idea. We were asked to not come back. That served to shake our foundation enough that I knew we wouldn't survive. I let it go and it dissolved very quickly.

I had also been working with an organization called the Valley Riders as a mentor for some of their guys. Some conflict arose in their ranks and was not dealt with, so I decided to get out of there before it too fell.

The burden I had for reaching the MC world with the gospel still burned in my soul. I had been learning over the past several months to recognize God's

Birth of a Ministry

voice speaking to my spirit and I knew He didn't want me to give up.

There was a friend from Oral Robert's U. that I still kept in touch with named Sid. He was a true man of God. He knew the scriptures better than anyone I'd ever known and had a load of wisdom to go along with it. I mentioned my burden for the biker world to him in a phone conversation one day. He said I needed to meet his grandson, Joel. As it turned out, Joel was at that time prospecting with the Valley Riders.

I met him at one of the meetings and told him I knew his grandfather and that he suggested we talk. Joel was about 26 years old and looked like a hardened biker. He had his head shaved and wore a neatly trimmed mustache and gotee. His clothes were all black, right down to his jeans and leather vest. He carried himself with confidence and was quite intimidating. He rode a Harley with a custom, flame paint job, big ape handlebars and chrome spikes.

I was immediately impressed with him. He agreed to talk to me, but I could tell he was guarded. I began by telling him a bit of my past experience as a member of a Motorcycle Club. He eyed me suspiciously, but continued to listen. I explained how I came to know the Lord and about the ministries I had been involved with. Finally, I related the burden I felt for taking the gospel into the MC world.

His face lit up and he exclaimed that he had been praying for confirmation about starting a group that would follow the protocol of the MCs, but add to it a commitment to Godliness. We were instantly on the same page. We agreed to meet together and pray for God's direction.

We formed a bond as we studied and prayed and discussed how to form this group of men who would be totally sold out to the Lord, but able to fit in with one-percenters. He became like a son to me.

I learned that his road name was Wolf and so that is what I've called him ever since. He had known the Lord since he was a child. His Mom and Aunt had prayed for him and taught him from the Word right from the start. He had recently come back to his walk with God after a time of rebellion when he had been involved with an MC and worked for them as a collector. I knew, from experience, that he had to be hardcore to do that job. God had called him out of that life to serve Him. When I met him, Wolf was full of fire and zeal for serving his God.

I met a good friend of his, who Joel was named after, also known as Drilbit, his uncle Daryl, known as U-Turn and Wolf's close friend Ryan. They were all men of God. Drilbit and U-Turn were experienced bikers, familiar with the MC lifestyle who had had life changing encounters with Christ. Ryan was not a rider, but he was devoted to our cause and shared our vision.

We worked tirelessly writing down our goals and mission statement and establishing our by-laws. We founded the Blood Knights Motorcycle Ministry, formed to follow protocol and gain acceptance into the MC circles, to earn their respect, testify, to the glory of God, with our lifestyle, serve the community and share the Good News, as the Lord gave opportunity.

We decided that we would allow men to join who were not Christ followers as long as they agreed to live by the standards we set up. This fact set us apart from all other Motorcycle Ministries who only allow Christians to join. Established within our ranks is a sub-group known as Militis Christi, Soldiers for Christ.

Birth of a Ministry

This group consists of men who are completely dedicated to Christ by their words and by the way they live. We require officers to be Militis Christi, but anyone can prospect.

So, the five of us entered into this venture with excitement knowing God had called us, but not knowing what would come of it. Wolf was voted to be the President and I served as the Vice President. Drilbit served as the Sergeant at Arms and U-Turn as Road Captain. Because Drilbit lived in San Antonio and U-Turn in Austin the ministry started off with three different chapters. We met on a monthly basis and gave reports of the progress in each city. We also attended as many rallies as possible. Our reputation grew and we did indeed earn the respect of many clubs.

Word spread and we were contacted by several men who were interested in joining. We required them to read our mission and by-laws and sign a statement saying that they would comply before prospecting could begin. I shared my knowledge of the "code" between brothers with the group, while teaching them from the Bible how God says we are to live. Before long we had a good size group in Dallas and growing chapters in San Antonio and Austin.

After several weeks Wolf decided to move to San Antonio for a better job opportunity. San Antonio became our center of operations. I moved to S.A. a couple of months later. Wolf found a church in S.A. that was unlike any other church I had encountered. They embraced us and our ministry.

Now we run the security team for their very unique youth ministry. We serve communion to the congregation, in our colors. We organize events for the residents of the family homeless shelter supported by the church. We coordinate benefits to raise money for families struggling with medical bills due to catastrophic illness. We also own and operate a food and clothing pantry for people in need.

As for reaching the biker world; we are accepted and respected by the largest clubs in Texas. We have participated in rallies and rides all over the state. Wolf and I have been invited to speak and pray at many of them. We have seen a number of people, including many of our members, come to a saving knowledge of Christ and surrender their lives to Him. The ministry continues to prosper to this day.

◆ 22 ◆

Leaving a Legacy

WELL, THAT BRINGS US TO today. I am getting up in my years. Because of various health concerns I am no longer able to ride. Wolf is still the President of the Blood Knights, but I have stepped down from the position of Vice President. The ministry is going strong and there are many young men moving up in the ranks. I am proud of each of them and the men they are becoming.

I learned a lot from my involvement with the old school biker culture. My old club has become one of the largest clubs

Leaving a Legacy

in the world. Yes, they carry the reputation as one of the baddest, but when Christmas comes around everyone is glad to see them.

I know that I deserve to be in prison or maybe dead because of the life I led, but I am thankful to my Lord Jesus Christ that He had better plans for me. I still work with people struggling to overcome addiction, but now it is with a program called Celebrate Recovery. It is a Christ centered approach to the twelve steps. I am honored to have worked with some very special people and I am blessed to have had a part in many lives being transformed by the grace of God.

Most of my family has passed on. Blackie died before seeing me finish the steps, but I trust that God has told him of my freedom. A lot of my brothers are gone now. I will never forget them or the exciting times we had. Some are still in the club, some have moved on.

One became a banker, another a lawyer. One went undercover and is still around, somewhere. Delia died of an overdose and Roy went in a cycle wreck not too long after. Some died at gunpoint, others in bike accidents. One even became a priest.

I have met a lot of interesting folks along the way, especially when we were running security for the stage at shows. David Caradene, The Doobie Brothers, Tina Turner and Stevie Wonder are ones that come to mind.

People have asked me if this is all true. Yes, and then some. It would fill volumes of books to tell everything I have experienced in my life. There were good times and bad. Some people say I lived a life of pain, or a life of crime, or a life of failure. I say I lived a life of survival. All the things I went through made me the person I am. The only thing I would change, if I could, is coming to know God sooner.

Leaving a Legacy

The Biker world is run by a code that in some ways resembles walking as a true Christ Follower. They put great value on family and being willing to "take one for the team", don't be quick to write people off, be willing to forgive mistakes and learn from them, each of us is responsible for his or her own decisions, but those decisions affect the whole group, be willing to listen and learn from those who have more experience than you, actions always speak louder than words, material possessions are of less value than people and truth and knowledge are valuable and should be sought after. They stand with strength and boldness and perseverance. You can't live on both sides of the fence, so make your choice and live it to the fullest. These are all spiritual truths that are taught in the pages of scripture, but without Christ as your Lord they are in vain.

"Sprung From Hell"

It is my prayer that my story will inspire some of you to pursue God and come face-to-face with Him in the person of His Son, Jesus Christ, who gave His life so that we could have eternal life. Becoming a Christ follower is simple. You just put your trust in Jesus and what He did on the cross. Walking as a Christ follower is hard because it is the process of learning to be dependent on Him. After-all, He is God and we are not. If you truly seek Him and His truth you will not be disappointed.

My plans now are to retire to a piece of land I own and spend the rest of my days with friends who love me and share the love I have for our Lord. I will continue to serve Him till I am called home. I praise God for the blessing of allowing me to leave behind a legacy known as the Blood Knights Motorcycle Ministry.

Leaving a Legacy

My prayer is that this story will glorify God and lead some to a relationship with Him.

That's my story, and I'm sticking to it!

♦

CPSIA information can be obtained
at www.ICGtesting.com
Printed in the USA
LVHW091541051220
673432LV00002B/159